Infant/Toddler Caregiving

A Guide to
Social-Emotional
Growth and
Socialization

Second Edition

Edited by
J. Ronald Lally

Developed by
WestEd

for the
California Department of Education

the **Program** for infant toddler care

WestEd

Publishing Information

Infant/Toddler Caregiving: A Guide to Social-Emotional Growth and Socialization (Second Edition) was developed by WestEd, San Francisco. See the Acknowledgments on page vi for the names of those who made significant contributions to this document.

This publication was edited by Faye Ong and John McLean, working in co-operation with Peter L. Mangione, WestEd, and Tom Cole, Consultant, Child Development Division, California Department of Education. It was designed and prepared for printing by the staff of CDE Press, with the cover and interior design created and prepared by Cheryl McDonald.

It was published by the Department of Education, 1430 N Street, Sacramento, California 95814-5901. It was distributed under the provisions of the Library Distribution Act and *Government Code* Section 11096.

ISBN 978-0-8011-1711-4

Ordering Information

Copies of this publication are available for sale from the California Department of Education. For prices and ordering information, please visit the Department Web site at http://www.cde.ca.go/re/pn or call the CDE Press, Sales Office at 1-800-995-4099. Sacramento, CA 95814; FAX (916) 323-0823. Mail orders must be accompanied by a check (payable to California Department of Education), a purchase order, or a credit card number, including expiration date (Visa or MasterCard only). Purchase orders without checks are accepted from governmental agencies only. Telephone orders will be accepted toll-free (1-800-995-4099) for credit card purchases only.

Photo Credits

Photographer: Sara Webb-Schmitz
Fern Tiger Associates (page 26)

Special thanks go to the following programs:

Associated Students Sacramento State University, Children's Center
Associated Students San Francisco State University, Children's Center
Chabot College Children's Center
Contra Costa Community College Early Learning Center
Covina Child Development Center
Eben Ezer Family Child Care
Marin Head Start, Hamilton Campus
Marin Head Start, Indian Valley Campus
Marin Head Start, Meadow Park Campus
Merced College Child Development Center
Solano Community College Children's Programs
Willow Street School House

Notice

The guidance in *Infant/Toddler Caregiving: A Guide to Social-Emotional Growth and Socialization (Second Edition)* is not binding on local educational agencies or other entities. Except for the statutes, regulations, and court decisions that are referenced herein, this handbook is exemplary, and compliance with it is not mandatory. (See *Education Code* Section 33308.5)

Contents

A Message from the State Superintendent of Public Instruction

S ocial and emotional development in the early years has become widely recognized as fundamental to children's early learning and development in all domains and for later success in school and in life. To address this critical area, five noted experts were brought together to create the second edition of the Program for Infant/Toddler Care (PITC) *Guide to Social-Emotional Growth and Socialization.* With a focus on temperament in early development, new research on early brain development, and the significance of close and secure relationships in the early years, this publication provides guidance on implementing high-quality early care and education programs.

Special attention has been given to the importance of building secure and responsive relationships with infants and toddlers and their families and of providing developmentally appropriate guidance to foster positive socialization.

Above all, this resource offers many practical ideas on how to develop nurturing relationships with children and guide their behavior and learning.

The suggestions in this publication complement the research-based descriptions of social and emotional development of typically developing young children that appear in the *California Infant/Toddler Learning and Development Foundations.* It is our hope that everyone in the infant/toddler field can use this new publication hand in hand with the other resources created by the Department to promote the well-being and long-range development of California's youngest children and their families.

Tom Torlakson

TOM TORLAKSON
State Superintendent of Public Instruction

Acknowledgments

This publication was developed by the Center for Child and Family Studies, WestEd, under the direction of J. Ronald Lally and Peter L. Mangione. Special thanks go to Stella Chess, Stanley Greenspan, Jeree Pawl, J. Ronald Lally, Ross Thompson, Janet Thompson, and Julia Luckenbill for their contributions of sections to this document; and Tom Cole, Consultant, Child Development Division, California Department of Education, for review and recommendations on content.

Emily Newton and Kelly Twibell are acknowledged for their thoughtful ideas and comments on Section Four.

Thank you to the following infant/toddler programs for allowing us to take photographs for this publication:

Associated Students Sacramento State University, Children's Center
Associated Students San Francisco State University, Children's Center
Chabot College Children's Center
Contra Costa Community College Early Learning Center
Covina Child Development Center
Eben Ezer Family Child Care
Marin Head Start, Hamilton Campus
Marin Head Start, Indian Valley Campus
Marin Head Start, Meadow Park Campus
Merced College Child Development Center
Solano Community College Children's Programs
Willow Street School House

Introduction

This document contains a wealth of information specifically written to help infant care teachers or caregivers with their day-to-day efforts to nurture social and emotional growth in infants and toddlers. This caregiver guide is one of a series developed by the Program for Infant/Toddler Care (PITC). The California Department of Education, in collaboration with WestEd, created the PITC, a research- and practice-based train-the-trainer series to support infant care programs in providing quality care. The PITC addresses all the major caregiving domains, from providing a safe and healthy learning environment to establishing responsive relationships with families. This guide to social-emotional development and socialization provides information that pertains to Module I, Social-Emotional Growth and Socialization.

The first part of the guide addresses three areas:

1. The Self: The caregiver provides physical and emotional security for each child and helps each child to know, accept, and become confident in herself or himself.
2. Social Skills: The caregiver helps each child feel accepted in the group, assists children in learning to communicate and get along with others, and encourages feelings of empathy and mutual respect among children and adults.
3. Guidance: The caregiver provides a supportive environment in which children can begin to learn and practice appropriate and acceptable behaviors as individuals and as a group.

The guide is divided into four sections. Nationally recognized experts approach the question of how caregivers can nurture early social and emotional growth. The information provided presents core concepts of the PITC that have stood the test of time. In addition, J. Ronald Lally wrote a new chapter titled "A Developmental Approach to the Socialization, Guidance, and Discipline of Infants and Toddlers." This chapter reflects content developed for the PITC Module I workshop, "Guidance and Discipline." Another chapter was contributed by Ross Thompson, who summarizes current research on key topics in the area of early social-emotional development: brain development, attachment relationships, and recent work on temperament. The two new chapters give up-to-date summaries of theory and research in the area of social-emotional growth and socialization.

Although each chapter focuses on the self, social skills, or guidance, the chapters overlap with one another by design. In daily practice, actions such as helping a child develop a positive and realistic sense of self, gain self-confidence, learn the social skills needed to cooperate with others, or follow social rules are not discrete caregiving functions. They all require flexible, individualized care based on responsive trust-building relationships. Each chapter, therefore, emphasizes and illustrates an attentive, responsive, and nurturing caregiving approach. Similarly, all the writers stress the critical importance of adapting caregiving techniques to rapidly changing developmental abilities of children as they move from being young infants, to mobile infants, to older toddlers. Thus, for example, J. Ronald Lally's paper shows how the caregiver's role as a provider and adapter shifts as a child moves from infancy to toddlerhood; Jeree H. Pawl's *gifts* become developmentally more sophisticated as children grow older; and J. Ronald Lally's chapter on socialization, guidance, and discipline explains how caregivers must choose different rules and limits to emphasize at each child's stage of development.

The appendix is a reprint of the social-emotional foundations that appear in the *California Infant/ Toddler Learning and Development Foundations* (California Department of Education and WestEd 2009). Based on current research, the foundations describe competencies infants and toddlers typically attain from birth to age three. For each foundation, a description of competencies is specified at three points of development: at around eight months of age, at around 18 months of age, and at around 36 months of age. In addition, behaviors are listed that lead to the knowledge and skills described for each of those three age levels.

One last point: Although an attempt was made to make this guide as comprehensive as possible, a decision was made to handle separately two major topics essential to the social-emotional development of infants and toddlers. Those topics are the role of the family and the role of culture. Because those important topics merit in-depth coverage, a guide on each of those topics is included in the series of caregiving guides. Those guides are to be used as companion pieces to this publication.

Section One:

The Developing Self

Introduction

*I*n the first paper, Stella Chess, M.D., explains how to recognize important temperamental differences, traits that shape a child's individual style of behavior. She defines and illustrates nine categories of temperament and discusses caregiving approaches best suited to them. Her comments have a direct bearing on the caregiver's role in the development of self and the need for a caregiver's understanding and flexibility in handling children with different temperaments.

Dr. Chess is Professor of Child Psychiatry at New York University Medical Center. She coauthored with Mahin Hassibi the textbook, *Principles and Practice of Child Psychiatry*. For the past 33 years, she and her husband, Alexander Thomas, have directed the New York Longitudinal Study, which established the importance of temperament in child development. In their work *Behavioral Individuality in Early Childhood, Temperament and Behavior Disorders in Children,* they reported the findings of their longitudinal study. This research significantly altered the study of normal child development and child psychiatry.

In the next paper, Stanley I. Greenspan, M.D., offers a picture of healthy emotional growth during a child's first three years. He charts for caregivers six different stages of emotional development, and he looks at the kinds of early experience necessary to nourish this development. In his paper he demonstrates the importance of providing physically and emotionally secure environments and underscores the role of caregiver as a model for the development of social skills.

Dr. Greenspan is Clinical Professor of Psychiatry and Behavioral Science and of Child Health and Development at George Washington University Medical School, Washington, D.C., and he is on the academic faculty of Children's Hospital National Medical Center in Washington, D.C. He is the author of *Intelligence and Adaptation*; *Psychopathology and Adaptation in Infancy and Early Childhood*; *The Clinical Interview of the Child: Theory and Practice*; coauthor with Nancy T. Greenspan of *First Feelings: Milestones in the Emotional Development of Your Baby and Child;* and editor of *Infants in Multirisk Families: Case Studies in Preventive Intervention*. Dr. Greenspan is also a practicing child psychiatrist and psychoanalyst.

Temperaments of Infants and Toddlers

Stella Chess, M.D.

Right from the start, babies are different. Each has his or her own way of showing feelings and of responding to the world around him or her. These differences, clearly visible in the first few months of life, are expressed in many ways. They can be uncovered by a caregiver who discovers:

- how active the infant is in body movements;
- how regular or irregular he is in sleeping, feeding, and having bowel movements;
- how easily the infant accepts a new food, person, or place;
- how long it takes the infant to adjust to a change in her schedule or surroundings;
- whether the infant's mood is mainly cheerful, neutral, or fussy;
- how sensitive he is to loud noises, bright lights, rough clothing, a wet or soiled diaper;
- whether or not the infant can be easily distracted from the activity she is engrossed in;
- how long the infant persists in giving his attention to any single activity.

Such traits make up a child's individual style of behaving—his or her *temperament*. Being alert to these temperamental differences and understanding how they require different caregiving approaches are crucial to nurturing children's healthy emotional growth. For example, you may discover:

- that certain children's "headstrong," seemingly cantankerous behavior stems from their temperamental slowness in adapting to new places, people, or games;
- that some toddlers are grumpy a lot and fly off the handle easily because they are unusually sensitive to loud noises and small discomforts.

A better understanding of how temperament works, especially when an infant's or toddler's behavior is exasperating, can help us maintain our own patience and positive attitudes as caregivers. It can also lead us to find the best ways to deal with such behavior. It is important to adjust our responses to fit a particular child's

3

temperament. A caregiving approach that works well with an outgoing, highly expressive child may be less effective, even harmful, with a placid or shy child.

The purpose of this paper is to help you recognize such temperamental differences in very young children so that you can develop effective ways of relating to children through their temperament that are best for them. Based on many years of careful research, my husband, Alexander Thomas, and I found that the behavior of infants and toddlers can be defined according to *nine categories of temperament*, which are identified on the pages that follow.[1]

Before outlining the nine categories of temperament, I need to emphasize a few general points about temperament and its handling:

1. No one made a full systematic study of these temperamental traits or their influence on the child's psychological development until my husband, Alexander Thomas, and I undertook a project starting in 1956. We started by gathering and analyzing details of the behavior of 133 infants averaging two to three months of age. (We have continued to follow these youngsters and are conducting a new follow-up into their behavior and lifestyles, now that they are adults.) In the research project, widely known among professionals as the New York Longitudinal Study, we found that the young infant's behavior could be defined and rated according to nine categories of temperament. Some aspects of temperament can be identified in the newborn, but in general they only begin to be clearly evident by two to three months and very definite by the end of the first year. Some young children show remarkable consistency in temperament from one year to another. Others show less consistency, probably because of the way they are handled by their caregivers and perhaps by differences in rate of brain development, just as normal children vary in the time and way in which they begin to walk or talk. Several research studies have shown a genetic factor in temperament; other biological factors, as yet unknown, are undoubtedly involved in shaping the newborn's temperament. There is no evidence that the parents' handling is the cause of the child's temperament. However, the manner in which the parents or other caregivers respond to the child's temperament may modify, or even change, its expression. Our findings of these nine categories of temperament and their importance for caregiving have been confirmed in recent years in different social classes and cultures by a large number of studies from several research centers in this country, as well as from various European and African countries and Japan, India, and Taiwan.

- Differences in temperament, even at the extremes, are differences within the *normal range of behavior*. All too often a child whose behavior is different from the average is labeled by caregivers and even by mental health professionals as having a behavior problem when, actually, the child is showing only his or her normal temperament. For example, some children are temperamentally inclined to move around a lot. This is a normal trait, not the pathological type of movement called hyperactivity. The key is to try to understand how that particular trait influences the child's behavior and to find the best ways of handling it.
- When caring for a child whose high or low extremes of temperament are troublesome, your goal should not be to insulate and protect the child from those situations that are distressing. That will only restrict the child's life and deny the child valuable oppor-

tunities of learning to master social expectations as other children do. Without such experiences children will not develop a basic sense of confidence and self-worth, which come from the proof in actual life that they are capable of coping successfully with the behavioral demands that their world expects of them. Rather, the approach to such a youngster involves finding what we call a "goodness of fit" between caregiver and child. There is a goodness of fit when you handle the child and make demands in a manner that enables the child to meet the demands successfully. When that happens, the child's development can proceed in a healthy direction. If, however, you pressure the child for a quickness and level of adjustment that is beyond the youngster's temperamental ability to achieve, there is a "poorness of fit," with the likelihood that a real behavior problem could develop.

- Do not blame the child if he or she is showing troublesome behavior because of a temperamental trait. The child is not being troublesome deliberately (to be malicious or spiteful). Also, do not blame the parents. They may not understand their child's temperament and may, in all good faith, be applying child-rearing rules that do not fit their particular child's temperament.

Temperamental Traits and Their Handling

In describing the nine different traits, I will emphasize the extremes in each case—for example, high levels of energy or sensitivity versus low levels—because children with these traits are the ones most likely to need special attention or handling. I will give typical examples of how very young children express such traits, and I will suggest the best caregiving approaches to take.

The majority of children display temperament at a level somewhere in between the extremes of temperament, and these children will fit into home or child care routines fairly easily. In this sense, temperament is similar to intelligence; that is, children of low, average, or very high intelligence may require special attention, and those of average or slightly superior intelligence will adapt to the routine school curriculum without great difficulty. I will also look at how these specific traits often combine in a child's overall makeup to form certain major patterns of behavior.

 Activity Level: Amount of movement and bodily activity

High Activity

The child who is highly active prefers games and play with a lot of movement; kicks and splashes in the bath, and likes to run around. Gets restless and distressed if made to sit quietly in one spot for long periods. Give a child with this level of activity opportunities for active play. If the group is engaged in some quiet activity, let this type of child move around from time to time.

Low Activity

The child with low activity prefers quiet games and can sit calmly, looking at picture books or coloring, for long periods of time. Because this child moves slowly, he or she is sometimes teased as a slowpoke. You should expect that it will take a child with this level of activity extra time to get things done, such as dressing or moving from one place to another.

Biological Rhythms: Regularity or irregularity of such functions as sleep-wake cycle, hunger, and bowel elimination

Regularity

The regular child sleeps through the night, takes a regular nap, eats about the same amount from day to day, and has a bowel movement about the same time each day. This child presents no problems with feeding or sleeping schedules and is usually toilet trained easily.

Irregularity

In contrast to the regular child, this one varies in sleep habits and hunger patterns, and he may wake up several times at night. The irregular child's big meal may be lunch one day and dinner the next, and her bowel movements are unpredictable. You should accept this child's irregular nap and feeding schedules. The child can be trained to sleep through the night if not picked up every time she cries. Toilet training will usually take longer and may not succeed until the child learns to be consciously aware of the internal sensation that signals a bowel movement.

 Approach/Withdrawal: How the child responds to a new situation or other stimulus

Approach

The approacher responds positively to a new food by swallowing it, reaches for a new toy, smiles at strangers, and when first joining a play group, plunges right in. Such a child presents few problems to the caregiver, except when this responsiveness is combined with a high level of activity. Then the approacher may run impulsively to climb a new rock or jungle gym, which he cannot really manage, or he may try to explore a potentially dangerous object.

Withdraw

Typically cautious about exploring new objects, the withdrawer is likely to push away a new toy or to spit out new food the first few times. Around strangers or when first taken to a new place, this child may fuss or cry and strain to get away. You should be patient with these initial negative reactions. Pressuring the child to make an immediate positive adjustment only increases his discomfort and makes it harder for the child to accept new people and things. Instead, small and repeated exposures to the unfamiliar let the child gradually overcome his early reluctance.

4 *Adaptability:* How quickly or slowly the child adapts to a change in routine or overcomes an initial negative response

High Adaptability

The quickly adaptive child adjusts easily to the family's move to a new home or a visit to a strange place. After only a few trials, this child accepts new food that was first rejected and is agreeable to changes in mealtimes and sleeping schedules. Such a child does not usually present problems to a caregiver. Occasionally the youngster may give in too early to unreasonable requests for change, such as a playmate changing the rules in the middle of a game. The quickly adaptive child may benefit from encouragement to "stick to your guns."

Low Adaptability

By contrast, the slowly adaptive child takes a long time to adapt to change or to accept something new that she originally rejected. Such a child is sometimes misjudged as stubborn or willfully uncooperative. A more accurate term would be cautious. Your approach should be the same as for the withdrawing child—being patient, giving the child a number of exposures to the change, and encouraging the child when she begins to show signs of adjusting. Pressure to make such a child adapt very quickly will only boomerang and have the opposite effect.

5 *Quality of Mood:* The amount of pleasant, cheerful, and openly friendly behavior (positive mood) as contrasted with fussing, crying, and openly showing unfriendliness (negative mood)

Positive Mood

Smiling and laughing often, the child whose mood is positive is easily pleased and shows it openly. Fussing and crying are infrequent. This positive mood usually causes positive responses in adults, who find it easy to care for such children.

Negative Mood

The child whose mood is negative tends to fuss or complain a lot, even at trivial discomforts, and cry before going to sleep. This child may show little or no open expression of pleasure, even at games or other events that please, but rather will have a deadpan expression. Be sure to spot such a child. While not ignoring the child's fussing or complaining, respond cheerfully to him. You may find to your surprise that although the child gives no outward evidence of pleasure at some special event, such as an expedition to the zoo, the child later reports it to his parents or friends as an exciting, happy event.

Intensity of Reactions: The energy level of mood expression, whether it is positive or negative

Low Intensity

The low-intensity child expresses both pleasure and discomfort in a low-key way. If happy, this child may smile or say quietly that he is pleased; if upset, the child may whine a little or fuss, but not loudly, or may say quietly that she is unhappy. It is easy to misjudge and miss what is going on inside the child if you take the mild reactions as evidence that he is not really displeased or upset. Remember that mild expressions may mask strong emotions. Pay careful attention to such expressions and take seriously the feelings behind them.

High Intensity

By contrast, the high-intensity child expresses his feelings with great intensity. When happy, this child bubbles and laughs; when upset she cries loudly and may even have a tantrum. In this case you have an opposite task: to evaluate objectively whether the issue is important or trivial and not be guided only by the intense reactions of the child.

7 **Sensitivity Threshold:** How sensitive the child is to potentially irritating stimuli

Low Threshold

The child with a low threshold may be easily upset by loud noises, bright lights, a wet or soiled diaper, or sudden changes in temperature. This child may not be able to tolerate tight socks or clothing with a rough texture. You should be aware of and attend to those reactions but not try to change them.

High Threshold

The child with a high threshold is not bothered by the same kind of stimuli as the child with a low threshold is. You should check regularly to see if the infant has a wet or soiled diaper to avoid diaper rash. Otherwise, this child may be content to suffer the diaper irritation because this child's high threshold keeps him from feeling irritated and uncomfortable.

8 *Distractibility:* How easily the child can be distracted from an activity like feeding or playing by some unexpected stimulus—the ringing of a telephone or someone entering the room

High Distractibility

The highly distractible child may start and look up at the sound of a door closing softly. As one parent put it, half the solid-food feeding went into the child's ear because she constantly turned her head at small noises or glimpses of movement. In the early childhood period, the tendency can be an asset to the caregiver. The child who is fussing at being dressed or is poking at an electric outlet can be easily distracted by showing her a toy or other attractive object. In older childhood, however, when persistent concentration on a task such as homework is welcomed, high distractibility may not be such a desirable trait.

Low Distractibility

The child who is not easily distracted tends to stick to an activity despite other noises, conversations, and people around. This is desirable at certain times, such as feeding or dressing, when the child's full attention makes him cooperative. But low distractibility creates a problem if the child is intent on trying to reach a hot stove and will not be easily diverted; the child may have to be removed from the situation.

9 *Persistence/Attention Span:* Two closely related traits, with persistence referring to how long a child will stay with a difficult activity without giving up, and attention span referring to how long the child will concentrate before his or her interest shifts

High Persistence

The highly persistent child with a long attention span will continue to be absorbed in what he is doing for long periods of time. In the early childhood years, the highly persistent child is often easy to manage, because once absorbed in an activity, the child does not demand your attention. However, the child may get upset and even have a tantrum if he is forced to quit in the middle of an activity—for example, at bedtime, mealtime, or departure time at a child care center. In such cases, you should warn the child in advance if time is limited, or you may decide to prevent the child from starting an activity that will have to be ended abruptly. The highly persistent child may also keep badgering to get something he wants, even after a firm refusal.

Low Persistence

The child with low persistence and a short attention span will not stick with a task that is difficult or requires a long period of concentration. If the bead does not go on the string right away, or if the peg does not slip into the hole after a few pokes, the child will give up and move on to something else. This child presents few caregiving problems in the early stages of childhood. Later, however, a short attention span and lack of persistence make learning at school and home difficult.

Three Major Temperamental Patterns

The nine temperamental traits obviously overlap, and they come together in different combinations in a particular child's makeup. We have found that in our country three special combinations of traits are most common: the easy child, the difficult child, and the slow-to-warm-up child.

The Easy Child

Typically, the easy child is regular in biological rhythms, positively approaches most new situations, adapts quickly, and has a predominantly positive mood of low or medium intensity. Such a child is indeed easy for the caregiver. She is easily toilet trained, learns to sleep through the night, has regular feeding and nap routines, takes to most new situations and people pleasantly, usually adapts to changes quickly, is generally cheerful, and expresses her distress or frustration mildly. In fact, children with "easy" temperaments may show very deep feelings with only a single tear rolling down a cheek. Such children make up about 40 percent of most groups of infants and preschool children.

Occasionally the easy child may have difficulty if he has adapted too well to the special standards of the parents, which then come into conflict with the outside world. For example, one child was trained by his parents to be meticulously polite and courteous at all times, with many expressions of "thank you," "please," "may I," bows and handshakes, and similar behaviors. However, in his playgroups he stood out as an odd duck and quickly became the butt of their teasing and pranks. The bewildered boy withdrew, completely frustrated. A clinical evaluation of the child and a discussion with the parents quickly clarified the problem. They were able to change their approach; the boy adapted to the new, more acceptable standards of his age-group; and he was welcomed into his peer playgroup.

The Difficult Child

The difficult child is the opposite of the easy child. The child may be hard to train to sleep through the night, her feeding and nap schedules may vary, and she may be difficult to toilet train because of irregular bowel movements. The difficult child typically fusses or even cries loudly at anything new and usually adapts slowly. All too often, this type of child expresses an unpleasant or disagreeable mood and, if frustrated, may even have a temper tantrum. In contrast to the "easy" child's reaction, an intense, noisy reaction by the difficult child may not signify a depth of feeling. Often the best way to handle such outbursts is just to wait them out.

Caregivers who do not understand this type of temperament as normal sometimes feel resentment at the child for being so difficult to manage. They may scold, pressure, or appease the child, which only reinforces his difficult temperament and is likely to result in a true behavior problem. Understanding, patience, and consistency, on the other hand, will lead to "goodness of fit," with a final positive adjustment to life's demands. Then the positive side of the difficult child's high intensity of expression will become evident; the child becomes "lusty" and "full of zest" instead of being labeled "a rotten kid." Only a small minority of children, perhaps 10 percent, fit into the category of the temperamentally difficult child.

The Slow-to-Warm-Up Child

Finally, there is the group of children who are usually called shy. The child in this group also has discomfort with the new and adapts slowly, but unlike the difficult child, this child's negative mood is expressed slowly, and the child may or may not be irregular in sleep, feeding, and bowel elimination. This is the child who typically stands at the edge of a group and clings quietly to his mother when taken to a store, a birthday party, or child care center or school for the first time. If the child is pressured or pushed to join the group, immediately the child's shyness becomes worse. But if allowed to become accustomed to the new surroundings at his own pace, to "warm up" slowly, this child can gradually become an active, happy member of the group. About 15 percent of children fit this pattern of the slow-to-warm-up child.

Slow-to-warm-up children may be "invisible" in a group or slip between the cracks. They need attention and special handling to give them extra time to adapt. Then they usually make a wonderful adaptation. The key to working with these children is to go little by little, step by step.

A Combination of Traits

The three types of temperament just outlined are very useful to know in pro-

viding effective care for children, but they do not tell the whole story. The percentages given for the three patterns—40 for the easy child, 10 for the difficult child, and 15 for the slow-to-warm-up child—do not add up to 100. That is because some children's mixtures of temperament do not fit easily into one of those patterns. Furthermore, different children who can be called *easy, difficult,* or *slow-to-warm-up* temperamentally may vary in the way they express the individual traits that make up their overall pattern. One difficult child may be very irregular but only moderately intense, while another may be just the opposite, and so on.

Although we speak of difficult temperament in terms of the combination of traits outlined earlier, some children's care may be difficult for other temperamental reasons. A child with a low sensory threshold may be irritated by tight clothing, while other children with a higher sensory threshold will not be bothered. The child may fuss and struggle while she is being dressed and try to pull the clothes off. If you do not understand that the problem is sensitive skin, the child will be difficult to manage. In this and many other cases, there can be a difficult child whose temperament is not appreciated. Nevertheless, it is useful to keep in mind the notion of difficult temperament in terms of the combination of traits described earlier because children who exhibit a difficult temperament are most likely to require special understanding and handling.

A Final Word

If the caregiver observes the child's behavior in a number of situations on a number of days without making value judgments that label the child as nice, stubborn, aggressive, uncooperative, and so forth, it is usually relatively easy for the caregiver to identify a child's temperament, especially at the extremes. If the caregiver then adopts the approach that helps the child function in a healthy, desirable way, and succeeds with time, the change confirms the caregiver's evaluation. Many caregivers are able, even intuitively, to spot a child's temperament that is causing a problem of management and figure out how to deal with the issue, even though they have never heard of the concept of temperament. There are, of course, some cases in which a child's problem behavior may be caused or complicated by some psychiatric disorder. In such instances the caregiver's efforts may not be effective, and a mental health professional's evaluation may be necessary.

A child's temperament and the caregiver's response to it can be a highly important factor in the child's emotional development. The child's behavior with peers, relatives, and adults and the feedback he gets from them—as well as the variety of life experiences to which the child is exposed—all contribute to the self-image the child develops. If the child has discomfort with new situations, patient encouragement will overcome that initial shyness, and the child will gain increasing confidence in his ability to make friends and to master new challenges. If children who have intense negative reactions when frustrated learn that they get what they want if they have loud and long tantrums, their emotional development may result in their becoming "nasty brats." The highly active girl whose motor energy is channeled into useful directions will be pleased and happy with the approval this gains for her. If, however, she is left to her own devices, her physical energies may make her restless and even disruptive in group games, and she may be labeled a spoilsport and be scapegoated by her peers.

Thus any temperamental attribute may become either an asset or a liability to a child's development, depending on whether the caregivers recognize what type of approach is best suited for that child. The aim is not to indulge a child to become self-centered and fixed in his behavioral tendencies. It is quite the contrary. Having an appreciation of children's individual temperaments makes it possible to use the knowledge to help children mature into socially adaptable and welcome members of society.

Chart 1: The Temperament Assessment Scale

By answering the following questions for each child, you can increase your understanding of the temperaments of the children you serve. Refer to Dr. Chess's paper to help complete the scale.

1. **Activity Level.** How much does the child wiggle and move around when being read to, sitting at a table, or playing alone?

    Active   1   3   5   Quiet

2. **Regularity.** Is the child regular about eating times, sleeping times, amount of sleep needed, and bowel movements?

    Regular   1   3   5   Irregular

3. **Adaptability.** How quickly does the child adapt to changes in his or her schedule or routine? How quickly does the child adapt to new foods and places?

    Adapts quickly   1   3   5   Slow to adapt

4. **Approach/Withdrawal.** How does the child usually react the first time to new people, new foods, new toys, and new activities?

    Initial approach   1   3   5   Initial withdrawal

5. **Physical Sensitivity.** How aware is the child of slight noises, slight differences in temperature, differences in taste, and differences in clothing?

    Not sensitive   1   3   5   Very sensitive

6. **Intensity of Reaction.** How strong or violent are the child's reactions? Does the child laugh and cry energetically, or does he or she just smile and fuss mildly?

    High intensity   1   3   5   Mild reaction

7. **Distractibility.** Is the child easily distracted or does he or she ignore distractions? Will the child continue to work or play when other noises or children are present?

    Very distractible   1   3   5   Not distractible

8. **Positive or Negative Mood.** How much of the time does the child show pleasant, joyful behavior compared with unpleasant crying and fussing behavior?

    Positive mood   1   3   5   Negative mood

9. **Persistence.** How long does the child continue with one activity? Does the child usually continue if it is difficult?

    Long attention span   1   3   5   Short attention span

Emotional Development in Infants and Toddlers

Stanley I. Greenspan, M.D.

*T*oday, just as in past decades, some children grow into depressed adults and some feel fulfilled; some act impulsively, flaunt social rules, or take drugs; and others are responsible, respectful, and law abiding. But today, in contrast to earlier years, we know enough about how to treat children when they are very young that we can help prevent later difficulties and foster healthy personalities. Being aware of this emerging body of information, therefore, is of crucial importance to parents and caregivers of very young children.

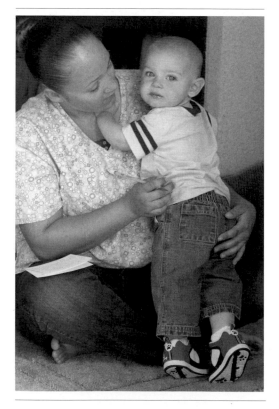

In *First Feelings: Milestones in the Emotional Development of Your Baby and Child,* I described in detail a picture of the healthy emotional development of children from birth to age four and the types of early experiences I believe are necessary to nourish this growth. As caregivers know, it becomes their task to provide those experiences when the parent is absent, but knowing how to do that can be very confusing. The $64,000 question is: "What can caregivers do to help infants and toddlers develop healthy emotional behavior?" I believe the answer must always begin with a solid understanding of the stages of children's emotional development.

Stages of Emotional Development

There are six basic stages in a child's healthy emotional development from birth to about four years of age:

Stage One: Self-regulation and Interest in the World (Age: 0 months +)

Stage Two: Falling in Love (Age: 4 months +)

Stage Three: Purposeful Communication (Age: 8 months +)

Stage Four: Beginning of a Complex Sense of Self (Age: 10 months +)

Stage Five: Emotional Ideas (Age: 18 months +)

Stage Six: Emotional Thinking (Age: 30 months +)

Stage One: Self-regulation and Interest in the World

During the first stage, which is from birth to about four months, babies are learning to take an interest in sights, sounds, touch, smell, and movement. Babies are also learning to calm themselves down. Even during the first weeks of life, as the earlier paper on temperament emphasizes, children respond to care differently. For example, some babies are especially sensitive. Note the following:

- Babies overly sensitive to touch will pull away and arch their backs.
- These same babies love a firm, gentle squeeze.
- Firm pressure helps them relax.
- Some babies are sensitive to high-pitched noises. In response to baby talk, they will startle. These babies do very well with low-pitched sounds.
- Some babies love to be moved quickly or whirled around in space. For others, moving too quickly is scary.

Babies are different, too, in their ability to soothe themselves or let themselves be soothed. For example:

- Some babies can, from day one, take their fist, put it in their mouths, and calm themselves down. Other babies cannot find their mouths.
- Some babies cuddle and nuzzle easily; others feel either too stiff or too loose. They cannot seem to get their muscles at the right tone.

In addition, babies differ in their abilities to understand the messages their senses take in. The ability to make sense of a caregiver's sounds, learned during the first two to three months of life, varies from baby to baby. Some babies can take in lots of baby talk and eagerly look at their caregiver for more. Others become confused by complex rhythms of baby talk and by fast talk, but if the caregiver slows down and makes only a few distinct sounds, the baby will understand and watch the caregiver's face for more messages.

It is very important for caregivers to detect these individual differences in order to understand the basis for each baby's developing interest in the world. Learn what is special about each infant's way of dealing with sensations, taking in and acting on information, and finding ways to organize her movements to calm or soothe herself; then act accordingly. What a caregiver does early in the relationship is important.

Stage Two: Falling in Love

By four months of age, babies are in the second stage of emotional develop-

ment, a stage in which they need to be wooed into loving relationships. Babies also differ in the ways they act during this stage. There are the more passive "laid-back" babies who need to be sold on the human world, and there are those who eagerly reach out and embrace their caregivers.

Caregivers who are not afraid to feel rejected and who do not take a particular baby's lack of interest as a personal insult can do the baby a world of good. Such caregivers can try many different "wooing" tactics based on a sensitive reading of what the baby shows he likes and does not like. Facial expressions, holding positions, types of touch and pressure, and sounds can all be used to communicate the experience of falling in love.

Stage Three: Purposeful Communication

By eight months of age, babies need experiences that verify that their signals are being read. Dependency (reaching out), assertiveness, curiosity, and even aggression are now part of a give-and-take, cause-and-effect pattern in which caregiver and baby "read" and respond to each other. Sometimes the amount of exploration and excitement generated by

new and different experiences during this period can lead to the caregiver overstimulating the infant, as in this example:

The new caregiver holds the infant's hands and wrestles his head into the infant's stomach. The infant pulls away. Instead of changing his action, the caregiver does it again, trying to get a pleasurable response from the infant. The infant pulls away again, but the caregiver keeps trying to get something going, almost as if he were playing with a dog or cat.

Experienced caregivers know better than to do what the new caregiver did in the preceding example. Experienced caregivers are usually involved in constant "signal reading." They know when to do more with the infant and when to do less. Neither overstimulating nor understimulating the child, these caregivers model purposeful communication. By respecting the infant's messages, they model respect of others for the infant.

Stage Four: Beginning of a Complex Sense of Self

By ten to eighteen months of age, babies need to be admired for all the new abilities they have mastered. They have organized their abilities into schemes to get things done and make things happen. The babies are inventive and show initiative, as in Wei's case:

Wei takes his caregiver's hand, walks to the refrigerator, bangs on the door, and once the door has been opened, points to the food he wants.

By acknowledging the child who completes such a complex action as Wei's, the caregiver contributes to that child's developing sense of self. When caregivers engage in complex play with the child and intellectually expand the play, they model new ways for the child to grow.

For example:

Wei chases you; you scoot around and double back on him. Wei giggles with glee and the next time scoots around and doubles back on you. Wei has increased the complexity of his behavior plan and his behavior.

Lots of imitation happens at this point in children's development, and so does the beginning of pretend play. By allowing for and taking part in early games and imitation play, caregivers help children expand their sense of themselves as complex, organized persons—of *me* and *not me*.

Stage Five: Emotional Ideas

By eighteen to twenty-four months of age, children are able to create images in their minds. Their pretending to be someone else is a sign of that, as illustrated in this example:

By cuddling his doll and calling it his baby brother, the toddler engages in fantasy. The two-year-old is able to create images in his mind's eye as if he were watching a movie of mommy and daddy, his baby brother, and himself.

During this fifth stage in the emotional development of children, caregivers can be of great help if they help children express their feelings as emotional ideas rather than just act them out. Make-believe play is wonderful for such expression because children begin to use words and gestures to label their feelings. Caregivers can provide young children with a safe way to put into words their curiosity about sexuality, aggression, rejection, and separation through make-believe play. The expression of emotional ideas is very freeing to a child but sometimes uncomfortable for adults. If caregivers find that they are having trouble letting children put those feelings into words, turning to other caregivers may help. As a caregiver, you may be quite comfortable allowing children to explore competition and anger but find that you cut off imaginative play about closeness and separation. By getting help with "hot spots" and "blind spots," you will open up more emotional areas to the child for his or her exploration.

Stage Six: Emotional Thinking

When children are about thirty months old, their emotional development involves shifting gears between make-believe and reality. In this sixth stage of their development, young children are beginning to have the ability to reason about their feelings instead of only being able to act them out in pretend play. During this stage of emotional thinking, setting limits and discipline become very important. However, limit setting must always be balanced with empathy and an interest in what the child is feeling. Here, too, caregivers need to look at themselves. Some caregivers who are very indulgent do well with the pretend-play side but are very weak on the limit-setting side; some who are law-and-order people do well on the limit-setting side but are very weak on the make-believe play and empathy side.

A general rule is that as caregivers increase limit setting, particularly with an impulsive child, they must increase the empathy and concern for the child's feelings and make-believe. The best way to encourage empathy is with what I call "floor time." This is one-to-one play where the caregiver follows the child's lead and encourages make-believe and friendly chit-chat.

Emotional Strengths and Their Development

When caregivers understand the six basic stages of emotional development, they have a clearer understanding of what they can do to help children in that development. I have found that visualizing how emotionally healthy three- and four-year-

old children function helps me decide the best ways to treat infants and toddlers so that they will develop healthy emotional behavior. In order to clarify your role in children's emotional development, I suggest that you review the accompanying list of qualities of healthy emotional development as part of your planning of day-to-day activities with infants and toddlers. Conduct your review with this question in mind: "Are my daily actions helping the young children I serve move

Healthy Emotional Development of the Child at Age Three or Four

1. Has warm, trusting, intimate relationships with other children and adults
2. Shows positive self-esteem: feels good about what she does
3. Uses good control of impulses and behavior; handles assertiveness, curiosity, and angry protests in ways that are in accord with:
   a. Society's goals
   b. Norms for peer group
   c. The settings the child finds himself or herself in, such as preschool, church, playground
4. Separates make-believe from reality and adjusts to the demands of reality
5. Exhibits a rich imagination:
   a. Incorporates and labels feelings
   b. Uses words to express needs, feelings, and ideas
6. Shows empathy and compassion for others; deals with loss and the limitations of life
7. Concentrates, focuses, and plans as a basis for learning in educational settings

toward emotional health now and at age three or four?"

After caregivers have a clear view of what constitutes healthy emotional development, they need to explore how children develop emotional strengths throughout the six stages of emotional development or how they develop negative traits instead.

Capacity for Intimacy

During the first few months of life, babies are beginning to take an interest in the world:

- The newborn pays attention to sights and sounds.
- By two to four months, the infant shows a preference for the human world.
- By eight months, that intimacy takes a more active form.
- By sixteen months of age, a child's capacity for intimacy reaches a new level. The child can carry a feeling of intimacy in his or her mind.

Based on memory of past events and through vision and hearing, children can understand gestures and even some words, and they can feel love from someone across the room. Children do not have to go to the caregiver and physically make contact, but they learn to feel close.

As children get a little older, they continue to develop the capacity for intimacy:

- By eighteen months to three years of age, the child has the ability to create images and emotional ideas in his own mind.
- Dolls can be made to put each other to sleep or to feed, to spank, or to hug one another.
- When the caregiver is temporarily in the other room and the parent is gone, the child can hold mental images of the loved one and not feel

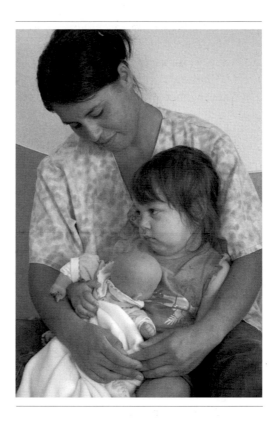

abandoned, even while the child waits for that loved one to return.
- Between thirty months and four years of age, the child learns how his feelings influence someone else.
- The child's intellect is developed enough to hold the idea that "being nice leads someone else to be nice."

When children's emotional development progresses as described, all is well. But sometimes caregivers will find that they have infants in their care who are not developing intimacy in normal ways. Some of the progressive signs that young children are having trouble developing intimate relationships are these:

- By two to four months, the child is looking despondent or sad. When the parent or caregiver comes into the room, the child may look indifferent and stare off into space.

- By eight months, instead of reaching out and gesturing "Give me a hug; I want closeness," the baby turns away, arches her back when approached, and prefers play objects to human contact. This child vocalizes, reaches, and moves but not in relation to the caregiver; rather the child responds in a passive, chaotic, or disorganized way, seemingly without purpose.
- By fifteen months, the child may not only avoid human contact but also bite or kick when someone tries to make contact.
- By eighteen months, the child may consistently refuse to be picked up and shake his head "no" or say no.
- By two or three years of age, the child is often either provocative and negative or passive, without spark, and does what she is told but without interest. *People are treated as things—no different from a toy.*

When caregivers see those behaviors, they need to pay special attention to the emotional needs of the infants and intervene through their own efforts or by seeking outside help.

Self-esteem

A caregiver can observe self-esteem blooming in the emotionally healthy four-month-old child who greets the world optimistically, and in the eight-month-old who vigorously explores the caregiver's nose, mouth, and hair.

During the later part of the first and most of the second year of life, infants' self-esteem can be seen quite markedly in their vigorous exploration of the outer limits of the family child care home or center. When caregivers enthusiastically join in the exciting searching games, the shared experience and mutual admiration show the child that his growing inclination to explore is something to feel good about.

It is important that toddlers admire themselves and feel proud of their actions. Those feelings develop when children have caregivers who can figure out what is special about each child and share their enjoyment of that specialness with her.

The three-year-old does not always need the caregiver to praise him for completing a puzzle. The child can imagine the caregiver saying, "Gee, that's a terrific job you did with the puzzle." The pride that the caregiver has so often shown becomes part of the child.

Limit setting by caregivers is also a critical part of building self-esteem. Children who are not secure that they will be helped to control their anger are often too frightened to feel good about themselves.

In helping children develop high self-esteem, caregivers need to understand what causes children to have low self-esteem, as outlined here:

- By four months of age, some children are already relating to people in a cautious way. These children show more than just temperamental caution. They act as though they expect to be rejected. Hector reaches out to the caregiver a little bit, looks, then turns away with movements and expressions that say, "I expect to be rejected."
- At eight months, when he returns to care after a weekend and sees the caregiver, Jamal looks away as if to say, "You're going to have to woo me back. Show you love me." If the caregiver is too sensitive to this rejection or too busy ("I don't have the time to bend over backwards for you"), Jamal's fear that he is

not loved might deepen. It is common for some infants to look away from a loved one after a separation, but the infant with low self-esteem makes "looking away" a pattern of relating.

- The fifteen-month-old child who looks sad or fearful and hardly ever insists, "Do it my way!" shows low self-esteem. Eighteen-month-old children who are so fragile that it is impossible for them to do things any other way but their own will do things differently only if threatened.

- By thirty months, some children expect to fail at everything they do. Sara knocks down the blocks before the tower is built. Vang messes up the puzzle before the puzzle is completed.

Impulse Control

As early as eight months of age, crawling babies will respond when a caregiver says, "Don't touch that!" They may look up and then go back to trying to touch it, but they listen. That is the beginning of behavior and impulse control. By the fifth time they hear, "Don't touch it," they may stop.

Even at eight or nine months of age, babies are beginning to learn about limits and controls. The caregiver helps by using gentle, consistent, and considerate words and gestures to let the child know what is allowed and what is not. By the second year of life, the toddler has learned to value and use that outside help to establish her own limits. By the time children are eighteen months old, they are quite capable of listening and attending to what a caregiver wishes them to do and not do.

When Dmitri wants to do something "bad," such as mark on the wall, the caregiver should let him know that it is not

allowed: "You can't mark on the wall. Here is some paper to mark on." Dmitri may see this as a game, but through the game he will learn to understand the caregiver's wishes and some of the rules people live by. Specific guidance techniques can be found in the paper by J. Ronald Lally, which appears in Section Three.

Words, gestures, and eye-to-eye messages, backed up by caregiver action when necessary, provide the eighteen-month-old child an opportunity to learn about limits. *But always balance the limits with time for spontaneous play.*

By three years of age, children will be using internal images to develop and understand rules. Caregivers can see this happen in children's more complex games and fantasy play.

Caregivers also need to be aware of the signs indicating that children are having trouble controlling their impulses:

- Healthy children will break rules, and they will challenge you. But they are continually learning, and caregivers can see their progress. Children who have not progressed may not be able to control their

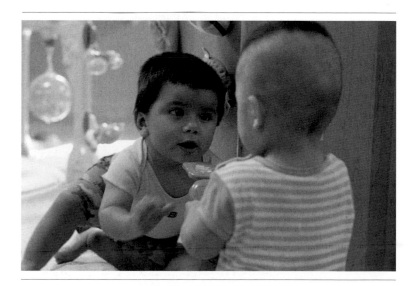

impulses because they do not have the foundations. They may have never learned at eight to fourteen months how to respond to limiting gestures and words. If they have received few limiting guidelines, there has been no opportunity to learn; for example, if they did something inappropriate and were simply ignored or pulled away with no clarifying words or gestures.

- Humans respond to cues that help them to know what is okay and not okay. If children have had much of their behavior limited (too much control), those children will break rules and overstep limits defiantly or sneakily because those are the only ways the children have found to express themselves.

Distinction Between Reality and Fantasy

How do children learn to distinguish what is real from what is pretend? The process begins with falling in love. To the four-month-old infant, the human relationship—with the parent and with the caregiver—is the carrier not only of warmth and security but also of reality. The child might wonder: "Where do I end, and where does the caregiver begin?"

"Who is doing the soothing?" The answers to those questions are very vague to the four-month-old baby. By eight months of age, the child has had a little more experience and is starting to learn about cause and effect: "I cry. She comes." "I smile. She smiles back." The baby's dependency is real, and so is the closeness of the relationship. For example:

- When a baby reaches out to be picked up, a human being has to be there who will read the signal accurately and respond by picking up the child.
- When a baby is interested in exploring and being curious, he needs a human being who will respond to that curiosity by saying, "Gee, you're doing great!"
- When a baby is being aggressive, looking the caregiver in the eye and pushing food off the plate as if to say, "What are you going to do about it?" the baby needs to hear how the caregiver really feels.

The eight-month-old child needs to learn that what she does will affect people differently. The child's anger, protests, and smiles all receive different responses. The child is also defining the "realness" of who she is. If the child who is reaching out to be picked up receives a message that says "Stop it, you're exhausting me, leave me alone," that child will come to define herself as too demanding. Those types of messages from caregivers can lead to confusion in a child: "Gee, I thought I just wanted a hug."

By ten months of age, dependency and closeness, assertiveness and curiosity, and aggression and protest are being defined. The child not only learns from the feedback that comes from caregivers of the reality of *me* acting on *you* but also begins to define what kind of me is acting on what kind of you. Reality testing, human to human, child to caregiver, is the way that children learn what is real and what they think is real about themselves.

The early reality testing ("If I reach out, I will be picked up") and its healthy development through the six basic stages of a child's emotional development lead to a child who, at age two, has a sense of what he thinks and how those thoughts relate to the real world. The child who has not participated in the reality-checking experience (with a sensitive caregiver who understands the need for accurate feedback) becomes either a child with a distorted sense of who he is and what to expect from adults or a child unable to distinguish very well between fantasy and reality.

An important job for the caregiver of the two- to three-year-old child is the ability to balance limit setting, reality, and make-believe. A caregiver who can play the role of the baby in the dress-up area, announce that it is time to eat lunch, set forth the rules, "You can't bite," and switch back and forth in the roles with little effort makes it easy for the child to switch from reality to fantasy and back again.

Imagination, Creativity, and Curiosity

The explorative touch of the four-month-old baby, the crawl to the distant ball by the infant at eight months of age, the climb to reach the toy on the top shelf by the twenty-month-old toddler, and the make-believe play of the three-year-old child are all part of the early work of imagination, creativity, and curiosity. But just what should be encouraged, and why? For example:

A two-and-one-half-year-old takes a stick and pretends it is a gun or takes a plastic gun and says "bang, bang." Is that good or bad?

Make-believe must be encouraged. Starting at about two years of age and sometimes earlier, make-believe play is a way for children to release and understand their deepest emotions. When make-believe play is allowed or encouraged, the child learns how to change the actions of hitting, biting, kicking, screaming, and crying into ideas she can explore. In other words, pretend-play should be thought of as the gymnasium for exercising emotional ideas.

For example, a child learns, through having dolls fight, to experiment with aggression in a safe way. Pretend-play also:

- helps the child get to the stage where she can say, "This is okay to do in make-believe, but it's not okay to do for real. It could hurt someone";
- gives the child a chance to learn to identify feelings;
- teaches the child to reason about anger.

The eighteen-month-old to four-year-old child must learn to take his feelings and move them into the world of ideas. He does so by using words to express feelings in make-believe play. Those make-believe dramas about separation, rejection, punishment, hugging, and feeding are the building blocks for emotional thinking, the ability to reason about feelings. Look what reasoning about feelings does for adults. The emotionally healthy adult can say, "I'm angry," and, reasoning about the anger, can look for other options. One option may be: "I have no reason to be angry. I'm just self-centered. That's why I get angry all the time." Or another option: "I have a good reason to be angry this time. I shouldn't be treated like this and I'm going to take steps to change things." If parents and caregivers do not allow for practice of emotional reasoning, children will get stuck at an infantile level of emotional expression. The older child may act out feelings as a much younger child might and get shamed or in trouble for those actions. An older child may also stifle feelings, as a younger child might, by restricting *any* release of feelings, including appropriate use of words.

Empathy and Acceptance of Loss

At about age three, a child will begin to say, "I feel sad. I didn't get what I wanted." Those feelings are expressed in play with dolls, too. Three-year-old children become more and more conscious about winning and losing. They express madness or sadness. Caregivers can help by giving children a chance to express how they feel about loss and losing and to "get into the skin" of others who may be feeling the same things, as in the following example:

> *"Oh, it's great for he-man Billy; he beat the other guy up. But how does the other guy feel?"*

> *"Well, I think he is sad, Mrs. Coffey."*
> *"Do you ever feel sad?"*
> *"I feel sad when I don't get a toy, or when I miss my mommy or daddy."*

Sadness is a natural and valid human emotion. It is an important emotion in learning to accept limits. Sadness is also the basis for empathy and compassion. A person cannot empathize with other people's sadness, loss, or hurt unless that person can experience those feelings himself or herself. Children can use the caregiver's help to "walk in other people's shoes." Giving young children the opportunity to see how their actions feel to the other person is a critical caregiving assignment. Not giving children the chance to empathize, or not modeling behavior for them to imitate, deprives children of one of the most mature emotions known to humankind.

The Caregiver's Role

This paper explains that children need the caregiver's help as children move through the various stages of emotional development. Children need to create intimate relationships, develop positive self-esteem, attain impulse control, define their sense of reality, expand their capacity for imagination, gain the ability to deal with loss, and learn to empathize with the feelings of others. In the past, much of the assistance in children's emotional development was provided in a hit-or-miss way. That assistance usually was not part of a caregiver's training, but many caregivers knew how important the help was and intuitively and naturally provided it. My studies of the stages of emotional development and the needs of children growing through those stages are intended to help caregivers who would like to pay closer attention to children's emotional development.

Chart 2: Baby's Emotional Milestones

I. Self-regulation and Interest in the World—Birth to 3 months

Increasingly (but still only sometimes):

—Able to calm down

—Sleeps regularly

—Brightens to sights (by alerting and focusing on object)

—Brightens to sounds (by alerting and focusing on your voice)

—Enjoys touch

—Enjoys movement in space (up and down, side to side)

II. Falling in Love—2 to 7 months

When wooed, increasingly (but still only sometimes):

—Looks at you with a special, joyful smile

—Gazes at you with great interest

—Joyfully smiles at you in response to your vocalizations

—Joyfully smiles at you in response to your interesting facial expressions

—Vocalizes back as you vocalize

III. Purposeful Communication—3 to 10 months

Increasingly (but still only sometimes) responds to:

—Your gestures with gestures in return (you hand her a rattle and she takes it)

—Your vocalizations with vocalizations

—Your emotional expressions with an emotional response (a smile begets a smile)

—Pleasure or joy with pleasure

—Encouragement to explore with curiosity (reaches for interesting toy)

Increasingly (but still only sometimes) initiates:

—Interactions (expectantly looks for you to respond)

—Joy and pleasure (woos you spontaneously)

—Comforting (reaches up to be held)

—Exploration and assertiveness (explores your face or examines a new toy)

IV. Beginning of a Complex Sense of Self—9 to 18 months

Increasingly (but still only sometimes):

—Initiates a complex behavior pattern such as going to refrigerator and pointing to desired food, playing a chase game, rolling a ball back and forth with you

Adapted from Stanley Greenspan and Nancy T. Greenspan, *First Feelings: Milestones in the Emotional Development of Your Baby and Child from Birth to Age Four* (New York: Viking Penguin, Inc., 1985). Copyright © Stanley Greenspan, M.D., and Nancy Thorndike Greenspan, 1985. Used with permission.

—Uses complex behavior in order to establish closeness (pulls on your leg and reaches up to be picked up)

—Uses complex behavior to explore and be assertive (reaches for toys, finds you in another room)

—Plays in a focused, organized manner on own

—Examines toys or other objects to see how they work

—Responds to limits that you set with your voice or gestures

—Recovers from anger after a few minutes

—Able to use objects like a comb or telephone in semirealistic manner

—Seems to know how to get you to react (which actions make you laugh, which make you mad)

V. Emotional Ideas—18 to 36 months

Increasingly (but still only sometimes):

—Engages in pretend-play with others (puts doll to sleep, feeds doll, has cars or trucks race)

—Engages in pretend-play alone

—Makes spatial designs with blocks or other materials (builds a tower, lines up blocks)

—Uses words or complex social gestures (pointing, sounds, gestures) to express needs or feelings ("me, mad" or "no, bed")

—Uses words or gestures to communicate desire for closeness (saying "hug" or gesturing to sit on your lap)

—Uses words or gestures to explore, be assertive and/or curious ("come here" and then explores toy with you)
—Able to recover from anger or temper tantrum and be cooperative and organized (after 5 or 10 minutes)

Later in stage and throughout next, increasingly (but still only sometimes):
—Uses your help and some toys to play out pretend drama dealing with closeness, nurturing, or care (taking care of favorite stuffed animal)
—Uses your help and some toys to play out pretend drama dealing with assertiveness, curiosity, and exploration (monsters chasing, cars racing, examining dolls' bodies)
—Pretend-play becomes more complex, so that one pretend sequence leads to another (instead of repetition, where the doll goes to bed, gets up, goes to bed, etc., the doll goes to bed, gets up, and then gets dressed, or the cars race, crash, and then go to get fixed)
—Spatial designs become more complex and have interrelated parts, so that a block house has rooms or maybe furniture, a drawing of a face has some of its parts

VI. Emotional Thinking—30 to 48 months

Increasingly (but still only sometimes):
—Knows what is real and what isn't
—Follows rules
—Remains calm and focused
—Feels optimistic and confident
—Realizes how behavior, thoughts, and feelings can be related to consequences (if behaves nicely, makes you pleased; if naughty, gets punished; if tries hard, learns to do something)
—Realizes relationship between feelings, behavior, and consequences in terms of being close to another person (knows what to do or say to get a hug, or a back rub)
—Realizes relationship between feelings, behavior, and consequences in terms of assertiveness, curiosity, and exploration (knows how to exert will power through verbal emotional communication to get what he wants)
—Realizes relationship between feelings, behavior, and consequences in terms of anger (much of time can respond to limits)
—Interacts in socially appropriate way with adults
—Interacts in socially appropriate way with peers

Chart 3: The Caregiver's Role in the Child's Development of Self

How to Help Develop the Capacity for Intimacy:

—Be warm and interesting.

—Be patient; position yourself so the baby can see you and is secure.

—Anticipate a baby's attention span for intimacy; before fussiness begins, switch to another activity, then later return to wooing.

—For a withdrawn baby, look for and respond to the baby's fleeting gestures.

—For a hyperexcitable baby, soothe and woo the baby with calming gestures.

—Woo the baby; let the infant learn about love from you.

—Set aside time for pleasant and loving exchanges.

—Tolerate and continue to woo a baby who is upset or protesting.

—Fine-tune your wooing efforts.

—For an excitable or fretful baby, become calm and subtle.

How to Help Develop Self-esteem:

—Admire the child's new abilities.

—Be a good follower.

—Determine a behavior that is easy for the baby to do; use the behavior for interacting.

—For a baby who is a low sender, react to any signal the baby sends.

—For an excitable baby, relax the baby and make the interaction relaxing and enjoyable.

—Bring the baby back to organized behavior when the baby is being disorganized.

—Help the child expand the complexity of her play.

—Recognize the child's need for balance between independence and security.

—Stay emotionally involved and available while you are setting limits.

How to Help Develop Impulse Control:

—Pay attention to which patterns help a baby recover after stress.

—Use those patterns, then stop to see if the baby tries to continue on his own to woo you and calm down.

—Help a child practice relating cause-and-effect interactions through language, and respond logically to the child's communication; do not ignore communication or change the subject.

—Do not let a child's aggression frighten you.

—Go "eyeball-to-eyeball" with a child when she is angry; help the child regain control; set firm limits.

—Reengage a child after an explosion.

Adapted from Stanley Greenspan and Nancy T. Greenspan, *First Feelings: Milestones in the Emotional Development of Your Baby and Child from Birth to Age Four* (New York: Viking Penguin, Inc., 1985). Used with permission.

How to Help Children Learn the Differences Between Fantasy and Reality:

—Gently introduce into a child's play an emotion the child avoids.

—Add logical sequences when a child's difficulty with an emotion causes him to make an abrupt shift in the story.

—Pay attention to how you handle any emotion with which a child seems to be uncomfortable.

—When the intensity of an emotion causes a child to become excitable or withdrawn, be alert to when the intensity is too much; provide more structure at that time to reengage the child; encourage the child to talk about her feelings; help the child put actions into words.

—Encourage a child to integrate opposite, emotional feelings toward one person.

—With the child who overindulges in fantasy, ensure you are providing enough security and setting effective limits; give the context for when the fantasy is appropriate.

—With the child who overindulges the reality orientation, look for family stress and lack of emotional support; gradually introduce the idea of fantasy into conversation and play.

—Make sure a child understands the functional role of objects, people, and feelings.

How to Help Develop Imagination, Creativity, and Curiosity:

—Allow a child to dictate how playtime is spent.

—Follow a child's lead in conversation or play.

—Respect individuality.

—Encourage the use of senses and movement in new ways.

—Begin with the activity a baby does best.

—Gradually add activities that encourage the baby to use other senses and motor systems.

—Through pretend-play, help the child go one step further in his story either by adding more characters to the scene or by shifting the concept of the characters.

How to Help Develop Empathy:

—Become a partner and provide both physical and emotional warmth during your playtimes; invite other children to play.

—If a child is not involved in emotional, cause-and-effect exchanges, use the child's involvement in pretend-play to woo her into those exchanges.

—Become the child's partner and gently introduce emotional themes into the play.

—Establish contact after a disruption. ("I'm sorry I shouted at you. I want to give you a hug.")

—Help a child to reengage emotional ideas. ("You know I get mad at you when you dump your toy basket. Why do you want to do it?")

—Respect a child's emotional intent. ("My, you look angry.")

—Provide bridges to help a child elaborate intentions in a more organized way; if a child has trouble expressing warmth, say "Come sit in my lap and let's look at this toy."

—When a child seems particularly sad, encourage the child to talk about feelings.

—Explain why you do not want the child to do something.

—Respond in an empathic manner.

—Support a child's understanding of the connection between ideas and feelings.

Section Two:

The Development
of Social Skills

Introduction

In the first paper in this section, J. Ronald Lally describes a basic caregiving approach called the responsive process. The caregiver's role is defined as a combination of learner, provider, and adapter. The responsive process helps develop the kind of nurturing relationships that lead young children to feel secure in themselves, value others, and learn acceptable behavior. In his paper, Dr. Lally points out the need for caregivers to redefine their roles in the development of the child's self and social behavior as children grow from young infants to mobile infants to toddlers.

J. Ronald Lally is Director of the WestEd Center for Child and Family Studies in San Francisco, which created the Program for Infant/Toddler Caregivers for the California Department of Education. The caregiver training system is based on DVDs, written materials, and technical assistance. Dr. Lally is coauthor with Ira Gordon of *Learning Games for Infants and Toddlers;* coauthor with Alice Honig of *Infant Caregiving: A Design for Training;* and coauthor with Kuno Beller, Ira Gordon, and Leon Yarrow of *Studies in Socio-Emotional Development in Infancy.* Dr. Lally also directed the Syracuse University Family Development Research Program, an early intervention program (from birth to age five) with low-income children and their families, and is currently directing the longitudinal follow-up study of the effects of the Syracuse program.

In the second paper, Jeree H. Pawl describes as gifts 10 particular ways of interacting with infants and toddlers. The 10 gifts illustrate the types of caregiver behaviors that directly influence infant self-esteem and model for the child how best to relate socially to other human beings.

Jeree H. Pawl is Associate Clinical Professor, Department of Psychiatry, School of Medicine, University of California, San Francisco, and Acting Director of the Infant-Parent Program of the UCSF at San Francisco General Hospital. Before moving to San Francisco, Dr. Pawl worked with Dr. Selma Fraiberg at the University of Michigan Medical School. Dr. Pawl is an expert in the assessment and treatment of developing relationships of infants, toddlers, and their parents. Currently, she is the editor of *Zero to Three: Bulletin of the National Center for Clinical Infant Programs* and serves on that organization's board of directors. In addition, she serves on the board of directors of several organizations concerned with the development and supportive treatment of families with infants and toddlers. Her most recent publications and research focus primarily on child abuse and prevention and preventive intervention with anxiously attached infants.

Creating Nurturing Relationships

J. Ronald Lally

For infants and toddlers to prosper in group care, caregivers have to form sensitive and responsive relationships with each child individually. Such relationships are important to children of all ages but particularly so to infants and toddlers. Your sensitivity and responsiveness as a caregiver strongly influence how each child in your care will act toward and feel about the other people around him or her. If you as the caregiver are reasonably responsive to the baby's message, when the baby cries, you come; when the baby acts shyly, you do not force the baby to make contact. You can give a positive tint to the lens through which the child looks at life.

Your responsive behavior as a caregiver has the following effects:

- The child learns at a young age that he can have an effect on the outside world and can make things happen.
- The child is encouraged to send more messages, to keep reaching out. The child will use and sharpen his or her communication skills because the child learns that communication works.
- The child builds self-esteem, learning, "I am someone who is paid attention to—I am worthy."
- The child's feelings of security, trust, and confidence in the world are nurtured.

Caregivers can learn to be more responsive by getting in the habit of following a three-step responsive process. These three steps blend into a natural "dance" that both the child and caregiver enjoy.

The Responsive Process

The three steps in the responsive process are *watch*, *ask*, and *adapt*.

Step One: Watch

Try to see the world in the way that a particular infant sees it. Do everything possible that will help you see life through the infant's eyes and feel life through the infant's skin.

Begin your interactions with any infant or toddler by simply watching the child.

By watching first and not just rushing to do things for the baby, you can avoid the mistake of reacting before you receive the full message from the child. Look with both eyes. Listen with both ears. Give the child time to get his or her message across. Watch for both verbal and nonverbal messages.

Try to get in the habit of constantly gauging the child's actions. Pay attention to all the channels of communication that are available to babies. Watch how they curl their toes, arch their backs, widen their eyes, wave their arms, and grow quiet. With older children watch their many gestures. For example, if children tug at their hair, sit apart from other children, or lie curled toward the wall, they are probably experiencing fear. You will be surprised at how much you can learn by watching.

In your daily contacts with an infant or toddler, you need to remember that *you must be willing to choose the role of learner* for part of the time. Only by first learning from the infant or toddler what she is calling for can you choose the right response.

Being a learner means spending a lot of your time observing, "reading" the child, figuring out what message he or she is sending—not only the sounds and words but also the facial expressions, hand gestures, and other body language. Sometimes learning means getting right down on the floor with the child and seeing things as the child sees them.

By observing the child you will see things that require your immediate attention, such as signs of physical discomfort or hunger. You will also get to know the child; you will find out over time what the child's special interests and preferences are and how you can build on those interests to establish a nurturing relationship. By being willing to pay close attention, by making this kind of observation part of your caregiving style, you will also discover the child's particular temperamental traits—how active or shy the child appears to be, what kind of attention span the child has, how adaptable to new things the child is.

Until you are willing to assume the role of observer while you are relating to young children, you will continually do things with and for children that are inappropriate, inaccurate, and sometimes emotionally harmful. Being willing to take on the role of observer is no guarantee that you will always make the right moves with a child. But because you are paying attention to the messages of the child, you will quickly discover what is not working and can try something else.

Step Two: Ask

After watching for a while, step back into your adult role and ask yourself how you might set up the environment—the emotional, intellectual, and physical climate; the social setting and your personal behavior—in ways that will assist the child the most.

When you begin each new encounter with a child, allow for the possibility that you may not know what the child likes or is like on that day. Ask the child with your movements and your words. Magda Gerber, the Director of Resources for Infant Educarers and one of the most highly respected trainers in the field of infant care, says we should take this role of asking very seriously:

> I go so far as asking the baby, the two-week-old baby or younger, "I see you seem unhappy. What can I do? I don't know what makes you unhappy, but I want to learn it." I think by asking, you invite the baby to give you the answer and be a partner.

Ask yourself: *What messages is the child sending? What are the emotional parts to the message—the intellectual, the physical, and so forth?* For example, you see that the child seems really to enjoy playing with toy cars. You guess that one way to engage or relate to the child might be through joint play with cars. One way to ask the question is to introduce cars to the relationship and see what happens. Also ask yourself: *What message am I sending? What am I bringing to this relationship?*

Sometimes you do not get a child's message because your own feelings get in the way, causing you to misread or simply not see and hear what is really happening. Part of tuning in to another person's emotional messages is being aware of your own feelings and emotional states. The more clearly you understand what is going on inside you, the more likely you will be able to read and respond appropriately to a child's signals.

As the caregiver you need to ask yourself about two kinds of feelings, those of the present moment and those from the past:

1. The feelings of the present moment include your level of energy and

your mood. Are you feeling tired, tense, irritable, or in good spirits? It is important to attend to your feelings and to realize that you are continually communicating them. Children are so sensitive to the adults with whom they interact that they pick up easily on feeling and tone.

2. The feelings from the past are more complicated because they come from your own childhood experiences. Often those emotional patterns continue to influence you as an adult even though you are not aware of the fact. If the past emotions are not

acknowledged, they may interfere with your ability to read a child's messages clearly and may even cause you to respond in inappropriate or harmful ways.

Becoming aware of how emotional experiences from the past affect your behavior in the present is an ongoing process that takes practice. Just by being willing to look at the connections between past feelings and events and present experience, you will bring a new awareness to your work. The following example shows what a caregiver named Carol learned about herself when she was willing to ask herself about the connections between her past and present experience:

Carol began to notice that she was bothered by a child who had a tendency to tease the younger children, provoking them and taking away their toys. She also noticed how intensely the child's actions irritated and angered her. She could not stand the way the boy acted. She saw that increasingly her interactions with the child left her feeling upset, worn out, and defeated—and she blamed the child.

Rather than leave things that way, Carol looked inward. Reflecting on her own childhood, Carol remembered how she had felt when her older brother used to tease and torment her by taking her toys away and hiding them—how her brother would laugh at her protests. When she turned to her mother to intervene, her mother most often would tell her to work it out herself. Carol experienced again those feelings of frustration, pain, and anger that had come over her when she had to deal with the situation as a child.

Sometimes, untangling your intense emotional reactions to a child or to a particular kind of behavior in children is very difficult. At such times you should ask for help from another caregiver or a supervisor. Another's view of the situation may shed light on "blind spots" and "hot spots" you carry with you from your own childhood.

When Carol became aware that emotional responses from the past were getting in the way of her care of the child, her feelings about the child began to change. She asked another caregiver to observe her and the child and to offer suggestions about different ways she might handle the situation. She found that second view very helpful. She realized that her current feeling of intense anger limited her ability to provide the child with constructive choices and had more to do with her than with the child.

Instead of being overwhelmed and upset in the face of the child's provocative behavior, Carol began to focus much more clearly on what was happening in the present with the young teaser and to devise strategies for action.

To be a sensitive caregiver, you need to learn about yourself as well as the children you serve. Your emotional reactions to different children and to certain behaviors are a big part of your care. Look inward and consider your feelings. Knowing your "hot spots" and "blind spots" makes you a better caregiver.

Step Three: Adapt

While you continue to watch and ask, engage the child. As you engage the child, you will collect valuable information. You may learn that the child does not like to share but does like to show things to you or uses objects to establish closer contact with you. You may find that the child wants to be left alone. Adapt your actions in accordance with what you learn: leave, show interest in what the child shows you, or allow the child to get on your lap because he or she seems to be asking for that.

Your action does not have to be in direct relation to the child. You may act on the environment to make it more interesting to the child—for example, put more objects on the floor—or you may try to interest some other children in peer contact. The point of your actions, however, should always be linked to your reading of the child. Watch carefully how the child responds to the conditions you have set up and the actions you have taken. Then modify the conditions or actions based on what you learn from the child's responses. Continue to learn and make adjustments until you feel you are providing what the child needs.

The role of adapter is the most creative part of your relationship with infants and toddlers. You need to look at the child's reaction to the hug you gave, the question you asked, the activities you set up, the decision you made to leave the child alone to see how he or she handled things—and adapt your subsequent actions based on the messages the child sent out in response to what you provided. Ask questions: *How close was I in my original guess about what this child needed? What is the message now? How should I change my behavior, revise the environment, or alter my opinions about this child based on what the child is telling me and on what he or she needs? How must I change conditions or my actions so that what I can better meet the needs of this child?*

Adaptation and Age

One reason continued adaptation by caregivers is important is that infants change so quickly. The ways in which you provide the care will change as the child grows from infancy to toddlerhood: you will move more into the background as the child becomes more competent to provide for himself.

Adapting to the Needs of Young Infants

The very young infant who is not yet crawling usually needs you to provide care in a physical way by bringing things to her—food, a clean diaper, objects to hold or suck—or by taking him or her to sights, sounds, and people, out in the sun, or next to a couple of toddlers. The infant also needs consistent loving contact with you—to see your face, hear your reassuring voice, feel the warm skin-to-skin contact. Consistent nurturance can help the infant feel confident that someone is there who will provide for his or her needs. Exactly how you go about doing that for a particular infant depends on the things you learn about the child in your day-to-day use of the responsive process.

Adapting to the Needs of Mobile Infants

The crawler, new walker, or young toddler, because of her mobility, can often go after what she wants. The child can come to you, go to food, and avoid things that are unpleasant. The young mover needs a caregiver who provides opportunities to

experiment and take risks in an environment that is safe, interesting, and healthful. At this developmental stage, you are not bringing the child to things or things to the child as often as you did with the younger child. Instead, you are arranging or creating environments and possibilities that allow interesting things to happen.

Your role is to set things up in the young mover's environment to make it safe and easy to explore. In that way you are automatically giving many confidence-building messages. When the environment is not ordered with the "mover" in mind, the usual caregiver message is very different: "Don't explore. Don't do things you choose because I do not have confidence that you won't get hurt or destroy things." The specific experiences and the kinds of environments you provide particular children must grow out of your careful observations as you interact with the children.

Emotional availability is also important here. At this age, the child often likes the caregiver to be available but not intrusive. You may have had an experience with a waitress whose eyes avoided your table so you would not be able to call her over. Sometimes you may withhold your full presence from children in the same way, afraid that being completely accessible will use you up or perhaps spoil the child. But you cannot read the child's signals or provide appropriate reassuring contact without attending to the child. So be generous with your attention. Unlike the inattentive waitress, let frequent eye checks say to the child, "If you want me, you've got me."

Think how wonderful and emotionally settling it is to the mobile infant to look up and see that you are there if needed. When your eyes meet those of the child and you send messages of love and reassurance across the room, you provide just the message the child is looking for. The unspoken messages to a child, "I'm here if you need me" and "I'm proud of your exploration," help to instill the confidence that the early toddler usually requires. What the child gets through this kind of emotional interaction is reassurance not only of the materials of growth (food, a safe and interesting environment, hugs) but also of your willingness to let the child choose and explore on his or her own: "I have confidence in your competence."

Adapting to the Needs of Older Infants

The older infant with good language and movement skills has the ability for abstract thought. Here your role shifts focus again. For your relationship to work, you have to understand that at this age the child is not only learning about the many choices available to him or her but also coming to understand that individual responsibility comes along with choice. The whole notion of individuality becomes central to the older infant's development. Having mastered walking, climbing, and combining words, the older infant begins to develop fantasy in thought and language as well as a feeling for past and future.

The child at this stage of development may see others as a barrier to getting what he or she wants but also begins to see the positive side of cooperation. The older infant often shows his or her developing sense of self by resisting others or saying no. The infant also takes pride in his or her own creations. The child needs a relationship with a provider who will support his or her curiosity, independent action, and creativity. At the same time the child needs tactful help to see how his or her curiosity, creativity, and independent action affect the people the child shares space with as well as the environment and other living things. You, as the caregiver, become a kind of sounding board by letting the child bounce off you his or her growing sense of what is acceptable or unacceptable. With the right sounding board, the child's creativity, curiosity, and independence continue to blossom while the child learns that he or she may not pour milk into the sandbox, destroy toys, or hurt other children.

The Evolution of Responsive Care

The more the steps of the responsive process (watch, ask, adapt) are practiced, the more responsive the caregiver becomes with the child.

The process of watching, asking, and adapting—the core of a good caregiver–infant relationship—happens hundreds of times a day. When you are truly tuned in to the children you serve, the process becomes second nature. You realize that watching, asking, and adapting are always interconnected in the daily give-and-take of caregiver-infant relationships. Once you understand the process, you blend the three steps into a natural dance that both partners enjoy.

Tips for Getting in Tune

Be attentively respectful. Observe without interfering. Spend time quietly looking and listening—leaving the child's psychological space intact—without interrupting or breaking into the child's activity.

1. Be an asker. Ask the child through words and actions what is right for him or her: "I wonder what is motivating Mei-ling?" "I wonder what Jose is interested in this morning?" Ask yourself: *Is what I'm doing meeting the child's needs?*

2. Pay attention to your own feelings. Gauge the part your feelings play in the relationship.

3. Keep in mind your own special emotional inclinations—your "hot spots" and "blind spots."

4. Watch as you act. When you take an action, watch while you do it and do not go too fast. Give the baby time to show you a response that you can learn something from.

5. See behind the action. Do not just see an action or behavior but see the reason and emotion behind the action. When an older infant scribbles on the wall, for example, she may be so consumed with trying out the new line-making skill that the infant may feel the act of making lines on any surface should be rewarded.

6. Use the information you have learned about children and child care—how children develop, how to cope with cultural differences, how to set up environments, how to use materials—to assist you in the adaptation process.

7. Pay special attention to what you have already learned from your interactions with each child in your care.

8. Use all the information artistically to create a unique exchange with each child.

Self-esteem, Security, and Social Competence: Ten Caregiving Gifts

Jeree H. Pawl

Caregivers take on a big responsibility when they care for very young children for long periods of time outside the children's homes. The caregiver is expected to be a competent and affectionate extension of the child's parents. The child learns to turn to the caregiver to meet his basic emotional needs. The caregiver has great influence over the picture the child begins to form of the world around him— that is, the child's impression of how he will be treated and how he should act around others. In instances in which the infant's or toddler's relationship with her own parent is inadequate, the caregiver's contribution to that child's sense of self and of the world is beyond measure.

Ten Caregiving Gifts

In this paper I present ten suggestions for care that I believe are some of the most powerful ways a caregiver can support infants, toddlers, and their parents. I call these *caregiving gifts* because of the great benefits infants and toddlers gain in self-esteem, security, and social competence.

Gift One: Respond to Very Young Infants in Ways That Encourage Them to Feel They Can Make Things Happen

The first gift the caregiver can give an infant is to respond in a way that encourages the infant to feel he has an impact on the world—that he can make something happen. Adults often are miserable at those times when they feel least competent, least effective, and most helpless. Babies are helpless in many ways—they are immobile and cannot fend for themselves—but they can let the caregiver know that they have a need. When the baby's communication of need brings a prompt and caring response, preferably from someone familiar, the response gives the baby the experience of having an effect, a sense of power.

The caregiver needs to respond when the need is expressed, not when the time is convenient or better fits the caregiver's schedule. One can imagine how good babies feel when the giants come running. Small and helpless as babies are, they can command and control what they need. Early infancy is not the time when adults need to teach children the limits of their ability to cause things to happen. It is just the opposite. By helping the young infant gain a sense of being able to cause things to happen, the caregiver creates a feeling of power in the infant and a beginning confidence in the child's sense of self.

Thus when a baby expresses a need for food, the caregiver feeds the baby but does more than satisfy the baby's hunger. The caregiver gives herself as a responder. The baby begins to trust that the caregiver is there for the baby, to expect the caregiver to be there, and to experience the pleasure in being able to get the caregiver to respond to the baby's needs.

Gift Two: Help Young Infants Learn They Have Ways to Take Care of Their Own Needs

The pleasure a child experiences in getting the caregiver to respond to her needs leads to the next caregiver's gift. If the caregiver always does things for a baby, the child will not have a chance to learn about her own competence. Therefore, another kind of power caregivers can offer to babies and toddlers is the power to learn ways to take care of themselves.

When a baby is mildly distressed—dry, not hungry, but "fussy"—the caregiver can speak to the baby (can the baby use sounds to comfort himself?), pat the baby briefly (can the baby pat himself?), and sometimes reposition the child. Perhaps with this cooperation the baby will find out that with the knees up he feels more content; or that while on the tummy the baby can find his own thumb. Next time the baby might move to that position without help. The baby learns that she can rely on things directly under her control. Again, the baby feels effective and competent.

This cooperation between the caregiver (as an alert and sensitive extension of the baby) and the baby (who can manage some things without help) underlies the growing sense of competence that is so necessary to the child's development of self-esteem. Many day-to-day experiences contribute to that complex sense, but it surely begins with caregivers both responding to babies' needs and providing babies with opportunities to experience being able to take care of themselves.

The process only works, of course, if the child's ability to care for himself is within the child's capacity. Otherwise, the child is overwhelmed, disorganized, and helpless. Here the art of caregiving comes in: *When do I help? How much*

should I help? When should I let the infant do things on her own? Occasionally, no matter what the caregiver does, a baby will experience helplessness and frustration. But if caregivers meet babies where they need help and let babies do what they can, the babies will experience an overall sense of control and confidence as a result.

One obvious way to promote a sense of competence is to offer choices to the toddler. That does not mean turning continually difficult decisions over to the child: "Do you want to look at a book, play on the slide, play with a puzzle, paint, or rest?" Promoting competence does mean listening to and granting the child his preference ("Go outside"). As the young child increasingly shows the interest and ability to make choices, promoting a sense of competence means increasing the opportunities for choice.

The caregiver may provide opportunities by setting up the home or center so that a variety of play choices is available.

When a child can move from one activity to another, depending on her mood and interest, the child will have a continuing sense of control over herself, the environment, and the expression of herself in the environment.

Gift Three: Help Infants and Toddlers Develop Confidence and Trust in Others

At the same time the baby is experiencing an emerging self-assurance, he also is developing a complementary sense of confidence in others. The baby is learning to trust that his needs will be noticed and that the world will respond. So, along with the positive sense of self, the baby develops the sense of trust in the caregiver. Trust is essential to how the baby feels about what she can expect from people in the world: Will people help? Will they hurt? Will they not notice? Should I trust people? Can I trust myself?

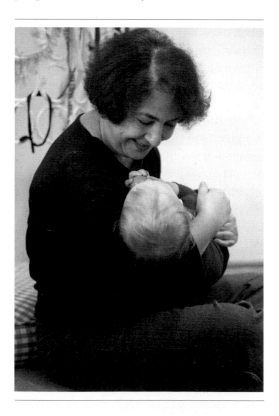

When the caregiver pays close attention to an infant's need to trust herself or another, the caregiver is not only satisfying the child's hunger or lessening the discomfort but also creating a confidence with the infant in herself, others, and the way the world behaves. That confidence is far more meaningful than the momentary satisfaction of hunger.

Astonishingly quickly, a baby begins to have expectations about what will happen when a need is expressed—who will do what to whom. Caregiver–child interactions work best for babies when the baby can begin to *predict* what will happen. For that to occur, the events must be familiar. The baby must be cared for in a consistent setting and get used to where things are and when things usually happen. When the baby is cared for by the same few people for months at a time, the baby becomes familiar with how the caregiver will treat her.

Babies can adapt to different caregiver styles, but not without some costs. Each caregiver:

- has her own personal style;
- picks up a baby differently from anyone else;
- picks up different babies differently;
- has her own unique voice, smell, and rhythms;
- is faster or slower, more vigorous or gentle than another.

Babies learn to anticipate those circumstances very rapidly. Within days, babies recognize the caregiver's smell, face, and voice.

If a total shift of caregivers occurs, babies as young as two months of age demonstrate their distress by having feeding and sleeping problems. To some extent the distress can be understood as a reaction to the disruption of the babies' ability to predict what will happen—they do not know what to expect. This example illustrates the problem: The disruption is like learning to dance perfectly with one partner and then suddenly being confronted with another. The steps you know do not work—the new partner is kicking you in the leg, and it feels awful. Your sense of control, the ability to predict your part in the dance, is badly damaged. You feel insecure and are not even sure if you can dance at all.

If one faces an endless stream of new partners, one may learn to dance with all of them, but one will always have to let them lead, and the lovely integration of partners will not be possible to achieve. In contrast, a dance with the same partner every time is personalized and intimate.

The caregiver predicts the baby's response just as the baby predicts the caregiver's: Two sets of eyebrows are raised almost simultaneously, a smile begins on one face, broadens on the other, the lips are pursed, the other smiles and bursts into laughter. Then the partner's lips are pursed again and the dance continues.

The imitations, the leads in even so small an exchange as a series of smiles and mouth movements are most meaningful. The wonderful ability of a caregiver to keep his face endlessly interesting and responsive to the slightest variation in the baby's cues is an internal, unconscious response. But the response is based on the intimate knowledge of the baby, on the ability to know without thinking what the next right move is.

Gift Four: Help Babies Learn About Intimacy

Intimacy or closeness between infant and caregiver can develop only when both have enough time together to know each other well. Babies are always ready for closeness when both have enough time

together, but they need a caregiver—or, at most, two or three caregivers—who knows them, likes them, and is principally responsible for their care. *More than three caregivers tax the very young child and dilute the quality and depth of the baby's relationships.*

Caregivers help babies develop the ability to engage in intimate interactions when caregivers do not stretch babies beyond their limits. The fewer the caregivers with whom a baby must learn to "dance," the safer the baby is from having his ability for intimacy overtaxed. Caregiving programs should ensure that no one caregiver has more than three young infants for whom she is the principal caregiver and that the infants are almost always the same infants. This practice will preserve the infant's capacity for closeness and intimacy, a capacity that affects everything that makes a baby feel effective, competent, and in tune with the caregiver.

Ordinary caregiving routines are special opportunities for closeness. These include:

- welcoming a child in the morning;
- feeding, diapering, cleaning the face and hands;
- putting a child down and getting the child up from a nap;

- getting a child dressed;
- preparing a child to go home.

Routines are not tasks to be rushed through but moments when the child learns that the caregiver knows and respects the child's likes, dislikes, moods, and fears. The caregiver's actions lay the foundation for a lifetime of such communication. Nothing could be more important.

Gift Five: Help Toddlers Learn That Adults Cannot Solve Every Problem

For the toddler as well as the younger infant, it is equally important to have a caregiver who is intimate and trustworthy, who knows the child well, and who provides for that child individually. The toddler stage is also the time, however, for the caregiver to move from readily meeting the child's needs to helping the child see that he or she has some desires

that the caregiver cannot and will not satisfy. The caregiver can expect the toddler gradually to show increased tolerance for delay and for the caregiver's inability, at times, to gratify the toddler's demands and wishes. An important caregiver role is to recognize and take full advantage of the toddler's rapidly developing capacity to accept the caregiver's limits to meet all the toddler's desires.

It is vital for toddlers to learn that adults do not have the power to make the world perfect. Sometimes caregivers can help toddlers appreciate adults' limits more easily than parents. Caregivers are far freer than parents from the powerful, passionate attachment to the child that sometimes pushes parents to present themselves as people who can solve any problem and always make the child happy. If they could, many parents would create a world for their child where everything was good and where joy, happiness, and contentment were the only emotions experienced.

Sometimes caregivers may lean in that direction, too. For the caregiver who feels that way and sends that message, a great tangle of emotions occurs when a child sees the caregiver as a source of unhappiness. What the child wants may be unreasonable, and yet the child behaves as if the caregiver is deliberately cruel. In such a situation, the following may result:

1. If the caregiver feels that he *should* make everything all right and cannot, the caregiver feels guilty. That makes the caregiver angry and soon what should be a simple "No, I'm sorry" is an angry "no" or worse.
2. If the caregiver changes her mind along the way and lets the toddler have what the caregiver's judgment says the toddler should not have, the caregiver runs the danger of agreeing with the child that the caregiver

is the source of all pleasure and displeasure. By doing so, the caregiver supports rather than weakens the child's notion that if the child feels bad, it is the caregiver's fault, and the caregiver could fix it if she wanted to. *It is vital that children learn that the caregiver cannot make everything all right.*

What is needed in this situation is another kind of dance, one slightly different from the dance with younger infants. The dance now shows the child that the caregiver will still give what is possible but that the caregiver cannot give everything—and some things the caregiver should not give at all. There is a gradual caregiving transition from the role of principal provider to a role that helps the toddler see that she, too, has some responsibility for her own feelings. This gift must be given sensitively so that the caregiver does not expect too much too soon and the toddler does not feel suddenly abandoned.

Gift Six: Be Tolerant of Toddlers' Internal Conflicts and Desires

As infants move into toddlerhood, they want and demand many things that are harmful, dangerous, or totally impossible. Caregivers occasionally frustrate some powerful wishes and are called on to satisfy the unsatisfiable. How caregivers understand and feel about those situations matters as much as the child's behavior does. The caregiver's feelings are quickly and easily sensed by the toddler, and the message the toddler receives about how the caregiver evaluates him at those times is extremely important to the toddler's development.

The toddler may express internal conflicts and desires:"I will be big. I will be small. I will be big-small!" "I want orange—no, grape—no, orange—no, grape—no, orange—no, strawberry."

It is easy to get caught up in this internal conflict, for instance, by fetching a series of drinks for the grumpy toddler, none of which does the trick. The drinks do not help because the toddler wants them all—some magical, multicolored drink that will fix the toddler's bad feelings. But those feelings really have nothing to do with drinks, multicolored or otherwise.

At such a time, the caregiver needs to recognize the child's dilemma, sympathize with it, stop the futile attempts to please, and offer a hug— essentially calling a halt to efforts to please. If the toddler refuses all juice, fine; the caregiver accepts the child's control cheerfully. If the child flings himself or herself on the floor, the caregiver offers sympathy and comfort but does not get caught up in the child's tantrum. If the caregiver can recognize, for example, that a certain toddler is out of sorts and that the toddler's insistence on having another cupcake is not really about cupcakes at all, the caregiver can offer that child comfort instead of exasperation.

The following example illustrates the importance of accepting and allowing the child's feelings:

When Sophia wants to explore the CD player that was brought in to play music for dancing, she has a fit when the caregiver stops her. The caregiver can admire Sophia's curiosity and acknowledge that her wish to explore the CD player and how it works is splendid. The caregiver can tell Sophia that she knows Sophia wants to play with the CD player. Of course Sophia is grumpy when she is not permitted to do so. The caregiver will not expect the child to always take such things graciously. Most importantly, the caregiver allows Sophia to own *her feelings.*

By accepting and allowing a child's feelings, even as caregivers control the child's behavior, caregivers help the toddler greatly.

Gift Seven: Help Toddlers Sort Out the Evaluations of Adults

When a toddler is angry and unhappy, it is often hard for the caregiver to acknowledge, without feeling defensive and guilty, either that she has caused the anger and unhappiness or that the toddler blames the caregiver for causing those emotions. Many times, because of the caregiver's discomfort, she wants the child to drop the issue quickly and be good-natured. The caregiver wishes that the toddler would stop expressing the pain and unhappiness the toddler feels because the behavior offers continuing evidence that the toddler feels wronged. At such times both the toddler and the caregiver will benefit if the caregiver can sort out the feelings for the child.

The earlier example of Sophia and the CD player shows that Sophia needs to know just what she has been told she should not do and what part of her action is all right with the caregiver. Too often, all of the child's behavior is treated as one problem: the curiosity, the disappointment and anger, and the resulting behavior are not separated. With that kind of reaction from the caregiver, Sophia is being asked to give up not only all her actions but also her feelings. As far as she knows, the feeling of curiosity that prompted her contact with the CD player was bad, her unhappiness was bad, and her grumpy behavior was bad. When the caregiver points out to Sophia exactly what part of the bundle of behaviors and feelings will not be allowed and what is all right, Sophia feels better. Through word and action, the caregiver communicates:

I think it is good for you to be curious. And it is natural for you to feel disappointed or angry when your curiosity is stifled. I want you to love your curiosity and treasure it as I do and know that it is all right with me if you feel disappointed or angry. What you may not do is touch the CD player while it is playing or kick me because I stop you from touching it.

When a caregiver does this kind of sensitive sorting out, she gives the child another precious gift. And the gift often makes the caregiver's own job easier because the child does not have so many things to be frustrated about. The sorting out:

- helps the child handle and tolerate feelings;
- helps the child learn what his feelings are.

By naming feelings, accepting feelings, and never demanding that children not feel them or not have some way to express them, caregivers create a mentally healthy environment for growth.

Gift Eight: Match Your Reaction to the Temperament of the Baby

Review the lessons from "Temperaments of Infants and Toddlers," by Stella Chess. Because the topic was covered well, I will not repeat the lessons except to say that accepting, rather than trying to change, a young child's temperament is central to the caregiver's role in building the child's self-esteem.

Gift Nine: Exchange Information with Parents About Their Children

Continuity of care is important to the emotional security of both infants and toddlers. This continuity is helped by the careful exchange of information about the child's development, the child's mood and behavior, and significant things that happen to the child. Also relevant is what kind of day the child has had prior to the moment of exchange of responsibility.

Taking the time to share the information ensures continuity of understanding and forges the quality of relationship between parent and caregiver that the child needs. The exchange of information works both ways. For example, a parent can let the caregiver know that Selena really did not want to come to the program today because no one could find her favorite doll that morning. The caregiver's awareness of the child's feelings will help to make a better day for both the child and the caregiver.

Gift Ten: Remind Children in Child Care of the Absent Parents' Continued Existence

There should be ready reminders for children in child care of their parents' continued existence. Pictures, items from home, and conversation about absent parents contribute to the children's sense of security about their parents' guaranteed return. For children who have trouble with the switch in care from caregiver to parent, caregivers can help by discussing when the parents will come and what the child might do to engage the parent ("Look what I made!").

Talking with the parent also ensures a less abrupt shift. The caregiver can help the parent understand the meaning of the behavior of the child so that a sensitive parent will not misinterpret the behavior. The following example illustrates a caregiver's response to a difficult transition:

"Brandon has really been missing you today and is giving you the cold shoulder so you'll be sure to get the message." The caregiver may suggest that the parent say, "I really wondered what you were doing today, Brandon. When you're ready, I'll be right here and we can go." That gives Brandon time to wrestle with his feelings, gives him control, and offers a way to approach his parent when he is ready.

This kind of help with transitions can avoid a lot of misunderstanding, hurt feelings, and perhaps the beginning of a bad evening. In addition, a sensitive response to the child who is having difficulty with transitions contributes to the child's sense of trust, security, and importance.

Conclusion

The caregiver who creates an atmosphere and a relationship with infants and toddlers in which the children are helped to feel effective, trusting, mutually engaged with the caregiver, personally known and understood, and the proper owner of their own wishes and feelings gives an enormous gift to the children and their parents. With this gift the children's emotional security and self-esteem will develop naturally. Caring for such children will be easier and more pleasurable. The caregivers will see the evidence of their dedication, understanding, and hard work in the healthy emotional development of the children in their care. There can be no better reward.

Section Three:
Guidance

Introduction

*I*n this section, J. Ronald Lally, an international expert on early childhood development, presents a development-based philosophy for guiding, and socializing infants and toddlers. His chapter focuses on the need to first understand the "developmental equipment" of each child being socialized as a first step in deciding how a child should be socialized. He suggests that rather than trying to come up with one way to effectively handle things, such as hitting or biting, we should personalize our guidance activities keeping in mind temperament, development, the social and environmental context, and other considerations.

Dr. Lally has directed child- and family-related programs at WestEd since 1978. He currently serves as Co-Director of WestEd's Center for Child & Family Studies, and WestEd's Program for Infant/Toddler Care (PITC). Since 1985 he has been the executive producer of 20 infant/toddler training DVDs that provide techniques to ensure secure and intellectually engaging group child care. He most recently co-directed the development of California's *Infant, Toddler Learning and Development Foundations* DVDs.

Dr. Lally is one of the founders and on the Board of Directors of Zero to Three (the National Center for Infants, Toddlers, and Families) and has been active in the development and operation of Early Head Start (EHS). He served on the Health and Human Services Advisory Committee on Services for Families with Infants and Toddlers that created EHS. He advised on the rewriting of the Head Start Performance Standards to make them more inclusive of the needs of infants and, once the program commenced, provided his two-week PITC intensive training to staff and leaders from all of the EHS programs opened from 1995 to 2004.

A few of his recent publications are "The Science and Psychology of Infant–Toddler Care: How an Understanding of Early Learning Has Transformed Child Care," The Zero to Three Journal, (November 2009); "Chapter Two: The Program for Infant Toddler Care" in Approaches to Early Childhood Education (Fifth Edition), edited by J. Roopnarine, and J. Johnson (Pearson-Merrill Prentice Hall, 2009); "How the Infant Teacher's Context Influences the Content of Diaries" in *The Diary of Laura: Perspectives on a Reggio Emilia Diary*, edited by C. Edwards and C. Rinaldi (Redleaf Press 2009).

A Developmental Approach to the Socialization, Guidance, and Discipline of Infants and Toddlers

J. Ronald Lally

The purpose of this chapter is to spell out an approach to the socialization of infants and toddlers that is influenced by a child's changing developmental capacities. Instead of focusing on how to handle a particular behavior—biting, hitting, saying no—this chapter deals with how socialization, guidance, and discipline techniques need to be informed by, and adapted to, the child's developmental capacities at the particular point in the child's life when the socializing effort begins. It explains why similar behaviors in children of different ages need to be treated differently. It also explores issues of context and explains why factors as diverse as adult-to-child ratios, environmental arrangements, and number of transitions in a program day

Note: Socialization, guidance, and discipline may be defined in many different ways. In the PITC's view, the following definitions are not the only definitions, nor are they unquestionably the correct definitions. The key point is that definitions should be provided to lessen confusion about recommendations that are related to them. The PITC proposes the following definitions:

Socialization and guidance: The sharing of rules for living through example, demonstration, explanation, and focusing attention.

Discipline: the enforcement of rules and the carrying out of consequences for violating the rules.

On the basis of those definitions, the PITC recommends that no discipline be administered until the child has reached the developmental age of fifteen months, because the child does not have the developmental "equipment" to comprehend consequences for the violation of rules.

can influence the behavior of the children in care.

The chapter begins by presenting how a child's changing competencies and motives influence the socialization process. It moves on to explain some of the ways an adult's "vision" of a child—beliefs about how children think and what motivates them—can influence how that adult socializes. It then discusses appropriate socialization goals for both individuals and groups and ways to prevent, or at least decrease, behavior problems. It ends with a section on how to plan and conduct individualized interventions with children.

Philosophy and Orientation

As infants grow, they become more competent. That is obvious. What is not so obvious is how teachers need to adjust their guidance strategies based on those growing competencies. Research (Brazelton 1998) has shown that during their first three years of life, children go through at least three major transitions in development: from the very young baby seeking security, to the exploring six- to eight-month-old, to the fifteen- to eighteen-month-old beginning to seek identity. These transition points change the way the child functions and call forth a different kind of guidance from the adults providing care.

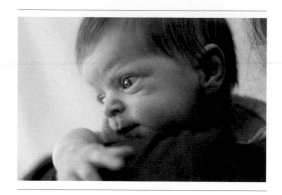

The baby
(up to eight months)

Because young infants have little capacity for controlling their urges and because they are desperately dependent on the external control provided by those who care for them, the adult's role in guidance in the early months is mostly to help children feel secure, help them gratify their needs, and keep them safe. When children are doing something their teacher sees as dangerous to themselves or others, the teacher gently redirects them, moves a hand, or repositions them. Much of what the youngest babies learn about how to act in the world comes from their experience of how they are treated by their caregivers. Babies observe and absorb. Your modeling of kindness and provision of protection and nurturance are powerful teachers.

The explorer
(six to eighteen months)

When children reach the age of six or seven months, both physical and mental equipment change. These babies become more and more interested in leaving the nest and exploring. They are changing the way they need you to provide security. They want you to be available and attentive but not doing everything for them. Maybe these explorers are just starting to crawl or trying to position arms, legs, and bodies to examine things of inter-

est. Children of this age start to take over some of the regulation of their bodies, moving toward things they desire and persisting with attempts at more complex movements. They wait a little bit for their bottle or decrease their crying when they see that their caregiver is on the way (Fox and Calkins 2003). They are gaining some control and exhibiting new developmental skills that need to be acknowledged. Although they certainly are not in control of their impulses, they are showing a growing level of control. How these children should be socialized changes slightly from how the very young infant was socialized. With these children, you can demonstrate more, briefly explain things, and use their interest in exploration to focus or refocus their attention (Scaramella and Leve 2004).

A child of this age drops a spoon to see where it goes or turns on the TV 15 times in a row to cause the colors and sounds to come on, not to drive you crazy, but to explore. Because children are motivated by discovery rather than defiance, demonstration, brief explanation, and focusing attention work well at this age, as does giving them some space to explore.

The individual
(fifteen to thirty-six months)

At around fifteen to eighteen months of age, children reach another transition point. At this age children begin to show the emergence of an understanding of the concepts of *me* and *mine*. They exhibit a forceful standing on their own two feet and also an understanding of the power of choice. This period in life is when children learn how they are to consider their needs and wants as they relate to the needs and wants of others. These children can move fast. They understand lots of words, and they know how to do many things. And because they are gaining these skills, society expects more of them (Fox and Calkins 2003). For example, they are expected to share and to be quiet in church or public gatherings. Often they react to these affronts to their freedom by saying no. This resistance is part of this new period of development. Through resistance they explore a new understanding of self and other—both a liberating and scary discovery. Clearly they are different in both capability and motive from the younger explorer.

With regard to guidance of children this age, your behavior should change as children change. These children have greater physical, social, language, and intellectual capabilities. They can make conscious choices. They can strategize to get their way. They can feel shame and pride (Lewis, Alessandri, and Sullivan 1992). Therefore, you need to take these new skills and motives into consideration as you provide guidance. At this point in development guidance, techniques should

expand to include culturally sensitive rules for behavior (Denham 1998) and consequences for the transgression of rules. In addition to continuing the socialization and guidance techniques already discussed for use with the younger infant, you can now add some simple rules for behavior—for example, no physical aggression toward other living things, no destruction of property. Why? Because children now have the developmental sophistication to begin to understand rules and the consequences related to the breaking of rules. See the box below for some suggestions with toddlers.

Tips for Guiding Older Infants

Have a Long-Range Goal in Mind
Optimize the development of feelings of personal security, confidence, initiative, and usefulness in children while simultaneously instilling a sense of self-regulation, a deep connection with fellow humans and other living things, and a reverence for the planet.

Understand the Role of Arbiter of Culturally Appropriate Behavior
It is important to understand that children naturally look to caregivers as the arbiter of culturally appropriate behavior. *Accept this role.* It is part of the human experience. *Do not abuse this role.* You are setting the child on a path of interaction with others.

Create a Lawful Climate
Make sure that the individuation experiences and socialization lessons take place in a lawful and orderly environment. The rules for behavior are clear and fair and consistently enforced in specific and reasoned ways.

Make Evident the Contributions of Each Child to the Group

Part of learning appropriate boundaries to one's actions in a group is coming to the awareness of one's value to the larger group. An adult's pointing out and appreciating a child's inclination to contribute and be useful to the group is essential.

Be Specific

Point out specifically those parts of a child's behavior that are the ones that need to be regulated and those that do not. Be clear enough in your message that the child cannot generalize to other components of the behavior that do not need to be regulated.

Do Not Give Up

It may take months of help for a child to shape a socially inappropriate behavior into a more socially appropriate one. Look for little steps along the way and point them out to the child when you see them. Additionally, careful design of the environment, identification of children's feelings, and extra supervision of emotionally charged interactions can help the child along the way.

Making the Shift

The ability of teachers to shift the way they socialize based on the child's point in development is a key to effective guidance. Learning only one way to handle biting, hitting, or anything else does not work. It does not make sense to speak of "feeding problems," "sleep problems," or "negative behavior" as if they were distinct categories. Rather, teachers need to search for the meaning of feeding and sleep disturbances or behavior disorders in the developmental phase that has produced them.

Teachers need to learn to shift their techniques as the child develops. Not doing so would hold young infants to rules they cannot understand or assign to them motives for behavior that they are not developed enough to hold. For the older child, the practice would be to not set and enforce the societal rules that they need help with learning. Dr. Selma Fraiberg, a pioneer in the field of infant mental health and author of *The Magic Years*, put it this way:

> We can see that a method that is indicated for one stage of development may be completely unsuited for another stage of development. For example, the principle underlying our care of the infant in the first few months is one of total gratification of need. But if we apply this principle to the rearing of the two year old or the still older child we would be rearing an extremely dependent, ill-mannered child. The difference clearly is the equipment of the infant and equipment of the older child. (1959, 75)

One of the biggest mistakes that parents and teachers can make while socializing a child is inappropriate reading of motive. If you treat an eleven-month-old baby as if he had the developmental skills and motives of an older toddler, you will discipline him. If you conclude that the act of turning the light on and off ten times is a direct act of resistance, you will discipline the child for motives of which she is not capable. But, on the other hand, if you do not set limits for a twenty-month old because you still read the child as having the developmental sophistication of a twelve-month old, you would be doing the child a great disservice.

Dealing with the Period of Transition

Another mistake is not considering the disruption that can occur during transition periods. As children transition from one way of organizing their experiences in the world to another (from security, to exploration, to identity), children often display inconsistent behavior. This can be very taxing and confusing to a teacher. T. Berry Brazelton, in his *Touchpoints* work (1998), points out that during transitions the teacher must be extra sensitive to reading the child's cues; the transition can be upsetting to both the child and the teacher because what used to work to settle things down does not work anymore.

Dr. Fraiberg speaks of it this way:

A very large number of the problems that appear in infancy and childhood appear at the juncture points of new developmental phases. . . . Each of the major phases of development in infancy brings forth new problems for the child and for his parents. The emergence of a strong love bond between the baby and his mother produces a period of anxiety at separation in the child. The onset of independent locomotion, the striving for the upright posture, produces its own anxieties and typical behavior problems whenever body activity is interfered with. Body independence in the second year and the emerging sense of an independent self bring forth a period of negativism. The cultural demands of weaning and toilet training in the second year create their own problems for the pleasure-loving child who is now expected more and more to meet externally imposed demands. (1959, 75–76)

Plan socialization, guidance, and discipline techniques from a developmental perspective. Becoming aware of each child's current capacities helps you to make correct choices about how to

behave. Knowledge of children's major developmental transitions, the impact of those transitions on behavior, and the growth in developmental equipment guides you to make the right choices.

Setting Socialization Goals

Many adults automatically guide and socialize children in the same way they were socialized. The Program for Infant/Toddler Care (PITC) asks that you give careful consideration to the end result of your work. How are children to function when they exit the program? What are the socialization goals? The PITC has adopted a specific goal for the behavior of children who exit PITC-based programs: "a compassionate sense of wonder," and it is described in the box on page 57. Whether you use this goal or choose another for the focus of socialization activities is up to you. Please, however, spend time thinking about and clarifying your goals, because goals shape how you react to children's behavior. Also be sure to include the parents of the children served in the decisions made about how you will socialize. One area to consider as part of that planning is the area of

independence. There has been a great deal of confusion and cultural conflict about how a child should be socialized in relation to independence. This concept cannot be ignored.

The PITC postulates that a healthy sense of self includes three components of how children relate to others:

- Dependence—In some situations, children need to see themselves as dependent on others—understanding they can rely on the help of others and that there are others who are more powerful than they are to solve problems for them and provide protection and nurturance as well as guidance and instruction.
- Independence—In other situations, children need to see themselves as independent. As children become aware of the distinction between "me" and "not me," they need to find a culturally meaningful voice to express their choices, creations, emotions, and beliefs.
- Interdependence—In other situations, children need to understand that they are interdependent with other living things, seeing one's self

as connected to other living things. Complete definitions of self always include an understanding of self in relation to others and seeing oneself as part of a group. Children have to learn to consider not only their individual needs, wants, and desires, but the impact of their individual needs, wants, and desires on others and others' needs, wants, and desires. They also have to consider how their individual needs, wants, and desires fit with the goals of their cultural group.

In the development of self, one does not necessarily want to see as the socialization goal an evolution from the almost total dependence of very early infancy to a state of independence, but rather an evolving ability to exhibit dependence, independence, and interdependence in culturally appropriate ways (Suizzo et al. 2008). The PITC does not see movement toward independence as the necessary and ultimate outcome of development. Rather, it sees children gradually coming to the understanding that they have a repertoire of behaviors on the dependent/ independent /continuum, each of which is appropriate in the creation of a healthy self. Dependence, independence, and interdependence are a part of self from the beginning of life to the end of it and flexibly exhibited in mentally healthy individuals. As Jeri Pawl states, "It is that positive internalization of mutually respectful and contingent relationships that make this flexibility possible." Rather than value one component of self over another, the PITC seeks to help children learn the appropriateness of the full range of possible ways to define and express a developing identity.

A Goal for Socialization and Guidance

At the PITC, the goal for the socialization and guidance of children under age five is a concept that tries to encompass both the needs and rights of the individual child and the needs and rights of all other living things. This socializing goal is called **"A Compassionate Sense of Wonder."** This goal was selected because it is often seen that when people socialize children to be a particular way—curious, independent, empathic, obedient, altruistic, and so on—they get more than what they have bargained for. They want children, for example, to be independent but not so independent that they never rely on another for help or see themselves as part of an interdependent community. Similarly, they want children to be curious but do not want them to think that it is fine to take an expensive watch apart in order see what makes it tick. Living a life with a compassionate sense of wonder is a way of living that is curious but not destructive, thoughtful but not manipulative, confident but not overbearing, powerful and considerate, creative and responsible, and generous to both self and others. The PITC recommends that the socialization goals of a program should be framed in a context of "self in relation to others" rather than just focusing on a unidirectional goal such as curiosity or empathy. Behavioral goals should have the following four attributes:

- confidence in self
- intellectual curiosity and interest
- a sense of deep connection with fellow humans and other living things
- a reverence for the planet

Know Yourself

How you envision children dictates how children will be guided. What you believe about the capacities, needs, and motives of children influences the way you will treat them. Therefore it is important for you to be aware of the beliefs you carry in your mind about what drives children to action and how children should be treated. Your beliefs about who children are, how they are made up, what motivates them, and how they function dictate the way you will interpret children's behavior and react to it. If you believe children are a certain way, then you will feel that, to be a responsible adult, you must treat children in a way that is consistent with their nature. All of us have theories about the nature of children and act from that theory whether we are aware of it or not. The following box presents some commonly held visions of children that have been used as the basis for child-rearing practices in the United States. Look at those theories, compare them with what is now known from research about how children develop (theory VII), and see where you stand.

I. Natural, Unfolding Noble Savage

This metatheory comes from the early writings of Jean Jacques Rousseau and influenced, to varying degrees, Pestalozzi, Dewey, and Neil.* It views children as basically good souls that need to be protected from the damaging messages of society. The child is viewed as a blossoming flower—on a trajectory for healthy growth since birth. From this metatheory, a child's development can be damaged by too much interference from the outside. The natural urges of the child do not have to be controlled or shaped, nor does the child need to be trained to live in harmony with others. It is the job of the adult to get out of the way of the natural growth process and allow for the child's unfolding—and not to try to shape the child's behavior to meet societal standards. This "nature gospel" of education was quite popular in the United States in the late 1960s and early 1970s and inspired pedagogical methods worldwide.

I wish to wrest education from the outworn order of doddering old teaching hacks as well as from the new-fangled order of cheap, artificial teaching tricks, and entrust it to the eternal powers of nature herself, to the light which God has kindled and kept alive in the hearts of fathers and mothers, to the interests of parents who desire their children grow up in favour with God and with men.

—*Johann Pestalozzi* (Silber 1965)

II. Tabula Rasa/Blank Slate/Empty Vessel

The "blank slate" is another theory adhered to by many. The child is seen as coming into the world without predisposed inclinations. Starting with Aristotle and continuing with the writings of John Locke, this theory became popular in modern America through the writings of J. B. Watson, the father of American psychology, and in the late 1960s through the work of B. F. Skinner and the "behaviorist school." Many policymakers and politicians concerned with seeing that children obtain basic academic skills hold to this notion. From this point of view, the way a child turns out is completely based on the experiences the child has in the environment in which he or she is raised and information provided by others. All things, including child motivation, are produced, shaped, and molded by those in control of the experiences to which the child is privy. Under this belief system, those raising a child shoulder immense responsibility for how intelligent the child will become, how the child will express himself or herself, and how the child will act in relation to others. Little credence is given to the concepts of temperamental differences, inborn intelligence, or biological predisposition. Motivation to learn is often seen as the responsibility of the adult and not innate to the child. Because how a child turns out is to the blame

---

*A metatheory is a theory about a set of similar theories. It provides a conceptual framework for understanding theories with common principles. For example, the metatheory of the Natural, Unfolding Noble Savage encompasses the theories of Rousseau, Pestalozzi, Dewey, and Neil, among others.

or praise of those who raise the child, it is the adult's role to "write" on the "blank slate" or "fill" the "empty" child early and often with good and useful things, in other words, as much of the right content as possible.

> *There is no such thing as innate ideas; there is no such thing as moral precepts; we are born with an empty mind, with a soft tablet (tabula rasa) ready to be writ upon by experimental impressions. Beginning blank, the human mind acquires knowledge through the use of the five senses and a process of reflection."*
>
> *—John Locke, "An Essay Concerning Human Understanding"*

III. The Tempted (Devil on the Left Shoulder and Angel on the Right)

Many people bring from their religious training a view of the child as a being who is constantly tempted by competing messages: to do evil or selfish things or to do good or selfless things. Adults with this metatheory want to help the child to be vigilant to and resist temptation so that he or she can live a good and productive life. A key role in child rearing, then, is to keep the child from falling victim to temptation. Adults work to keep the child from temptation and remind the child that he or she will be tempted to do bad things in a constant struggle between good and evil. These adults see their job as reinforcing the messages of the angel and reminding the child to resist the tempting messages of the devil.

> *Be strong. The devil fights you. But this does not mean that you are sinful. Nor should his attacks shake you or confuse you. . . . Each time you repulse an attack of the devil you secure a victory and you gratify God. . . . Thus the temptations force the evil that is hiding in us to come to the surface. The temptations arise from the flesh, the world, and the devil.*
>
> *—St. Theophan the Recluse*

IV. Unsocialized Savage

This metatheory comes from Puritan writings and beliefs. From this point of view, unless impulses are strongly inhibited and controlled from birth, the child will continue into adulthood as an unsocialized and uncivilized being. Early urges, if not checked, will create an adult who is too sexual, is unethical, and is greedy—someone who seeks only personal pleasure and gain. Thus, it is the duty of the responsible adult to control the child's willfulness and stifle acting-out urges with stern, powerful, and consistent discipline. This way of viewing the child leads adults to practices that are aimed at nipping expected bad behavior in the bud. Feeding on schedule, letting a child cry things out, not "spoiling," and clear messages of adult control are techniques often used by those who adhere to this theory. Child rearing is seen as a fight for power between child and adult right from the beginning of life.

Therefore, adult control of child behavior should start as early as possible so that self-will can be broken and the child kept from a destructive developmental trajectory.

> *Every man born into the world now bears the image of the devil, in pride and will, the image of the beast, in sensual appetites and desires.*
>
> —*John Wesley* (Greven 1988, 64)

V. The Early Unformed

Many people look at infants and do not see anything but an eating, sleeping, and defecating machine. They see in the child no intellectual activity, no awareness of feelings, and little need for social contact. They believe that the child is not capable of conscious activity until he or she has grown out of the infancy period. Statements about child rearing from this point of view follow this pattern: "Why would anyone talk to infants, interact with them, consider their feelings—they can't understand you." The adult who believes that the infant or young child has few feelings and does not register much about what is going on feels free to do most anything in the child's presence or to leave the child alone for long periods. Loud televisions, screaming fights within earshot, or isolation in a crib or playpen are seen as having no effect on the child because the child registers little. Pretty much anything can happen (or not) without permanent consequence to the very young child. Many fathers who hold this metatheory delay relating to their child until the child is about two and seems to have developed sufficiently to demonstrably need or benefit from engagement.

> *In fact, the baby (for both Freud and Lacan) is a kind of blob, with no sense of self or individuated identity, and no sense even of its body as a coherent unified whole. This baby-blob is driven by NEED; it needs food, it needs comfort/ safety, it needs to be changed, etc. These needs are satisfiable, and can be satisfied by an object. When the baby needs food, it gets a breast (or a bottle); when it needs safety, it gets hugged. The baby, in this state of NEED, doesn't recognize any distinction between itself and the objects that meet its needs; it doesn't recognize that an object (like a breast) is part of another whole person (because it doesn't have any concept yet of "whole person"). There's no distinction between it and anyone or anything else; there are only needs and things that satisfy those needs.*
>
> —*Dr. Mary Klages,* "Lectures on Jacques Lacan"

VI. The Innocent

In many cultures, children are seen as innocent and unmotivated by inappropriate thoughts and feelings until they reach their fifth, sixth, or seventh birthday. This theory postulates that until reaching this "age of reason," the child should not be held responsible for right or wrong actions. Before reaching the age of reason, the child is seen as not having the developmental equipment to operate from manipulative motives. Adults who view the young child as an innocent often give the child free rein to explore, to choose how and with what to play, and to "be a child." Once the child reaches the age of reason, however, things change dramatically. Adults' expectations for responsible behavior shift suddenly, and so do discipline techniques and education practices. At this transition point, children are held accountable, and school becomes a much more serious business.

> *The age of discretion both for confession and for communion is the age in which the child begins to reason, i.e., around the seventh year, either before or after. From that time begins the obligation of satisfying both the precept of confession and of communion.*
>
> —*A Letter from the Vatican: March 31, 1977,*
> *First Penance, First Communion*
> (Knox and Wright 1977)

VII. The Competent/Vulnerable Child

This metatheory, based on recent analyses of research on child growth and development, paints the young child as simultaneously wearing two hats—one that displays the child's vulnerability and one that shows the child's competence. This view sees the child coming into the world with a personal learning agenda and owning a brain that is genetically wired to seek meaning and learn language. The child is seen as biologically programmed to attach to, socialize with, and learn from those who care for him or her. This view sees the child as a curious and motivated learner trying to make sense of the world he or she is entering. While the child has skills, motivation, and curiosity genetically built in, the child is also desperately dependent upon adults for nurturance, support, and security. Without this adult support, the child will flounder. This theory, the one currently most supported by research, defines the responsible adult role as one of providing nurturance and support for the vulnerable component of the child's makeup while at the same time facilitating and respecting the child's skills and competencies. The adult who raises children from this metatheory acknowledges the child's biological predispositions to both vulnerability and competence and assumes responsibility for providing physical and emotional security while following the child's lead as the child acts out his or her social, intellectual, and language-learning agenda.

> *All children are born wired for feelings and ready to learn. . . . Human development is shaped by the ongoing interplay among sources of vulnerability and sources of resilience. . . . Children are active participants in their own development, reflecting the intrinsic human drive to explore and master one's environment.*
>
> —*National Research Council*
> *and Institute of Medicine 2000*

As the previous section makes clear, guidance encompasses a developmental perspective, appropriate goals for the child, and a better understanding of personal beliefs that may influence judgments and actions. This background leads to the next topic: prevention. Benjamin Franklin's old proverb, "An ounce of prevention is worth a pound of cure." is fitting in the area of socialization, guidance, and discipline. Much of the work in this area should be about how to minimize the frequency of inappropriate behavior. Making sure that caregivers are not creating conditions that provoke inappropriate behavior should be seen as a key component of the work.

Preventing Behavior Problems

The Environment

Setting up the program in certain ways makes it easy for children to comply with rules and interact with staff and each other and makes the day easier for everyone. Environmental arrangement, selection and distribution of materials, caregiving routines, staff and child assignments, and program policies are just a few of the ways to limit the occurrence of behavior issues. The shaded box on page 63 provides a list of conditions that do the opposite—increase the need for guidance and discipline.

Notice that most of these conditions violate the developmental needs of children who are three years old or younger. Careful study of this list may reveal things that can be changed in the environment and reduce the number of behavior problems.

With regard to the setup of the environment, things should be arranged so that children can easily figure out where certain types of activities usually happen and where certain types of materials can

usually be found. Dividing the environment into large-muscle, small-muscle, sense-perception, and creative-expression areas lets children know where certain things usually happen. The result is fewer interruptions of one kind of play with another and an easier flow of movement from one activity to another. Areas of the environment can also cause trouble. Look for narrow pathways and eliminate potential bottlenecks where children might have to negotiate ways to get past each other. The lighting and noise level, the number of objects on display, and the types of displays on the walls should be considered. Is the environment overstimulating to children? Calming it can help to calm the children. The heaters, windows, and floors need to be checked. Is the air fresh and invigorating or stuffy and filled with dust? These things can make a child grumpy by the end of the day. Are there too many toys out or too few? Having enough toys, but not too many, helps keep

children engaged and not fighting over the treasured one or flitting from one to another because they are distracted by so many. In a family child care home, precious objects must be removed from reach so that caregivers can say "yes" to the child's wish to explore rather than "no." This is true prevention work. Figuring out how to make better use of the environment and the materials in it can eliminate many conflicts.

Environmental Factors That Create Guidance and Discipline Problems

- Too large a group
- Too many children per teacher
- Too little space, too much open space, or a space that is cluttered
- Too few materials, too many materials, or not enough equipment
- Materials and equipment that are too challenging, too simple, or not child-sized
- Too much noise
- A schedule that devotes blocks of time for specific lessons throughout the day
- Too many transitions or too much change (e.g., caregivers, groups, environments)
- Inflexible routines and schedules
- Too little order or predictability
- Expectations for self-control that are too high (too many materials that cannot be touched or areas that are off-limits, excessive requirements for sharing)
- Too much waiting time
- Too much adult-directed looking or listening time; long or frequent periods of requiring children to sit still

Program Policies

Prevention begins with an analysis of program policies. Research has shown that if the program is structured so that children are in small groups rather than large groups, there are fewer behavior problems (Cost, Quality & Child Outcomes Study Team 1995). Caregivers get to know the children, and children get to know the caregivers and each other. Small group size allows the child to form relationships more easily and feel more at ease in a group. It also allows greater access to the adult when the child is in need of external regulation. A child-to-adult ratio of 3:1 or 4:1 also helps decrease behavior problems. Teachers are more available to each child and are more able to get to know the child well and to understand his or her unique needs and coping capacities (NICHD Early Child Care Research Network 1996).

Another policy that helps with behavior issues is the assignment of each child to a primary caregiver for an extended period of time. This arrangement allows the deepening of relationships through which teachers can get to know just how to relate to a child, the children know how to relate to their teacher, and the teacher and the child's family can work together.

Sensitive and Responsive Caregiving

There is also a great deal a teacher can do to prevent behavior problems by adapting his caregiving style to the needs of infants and toddlers. Below are some ways of acting that can either prevent or defuse behavior issues.

The baby
- Establish a positive, intimate relationship with each child.
- Spend some special one-on-one time with each child every day.
- Give consistent messages of unconditional caring.

The explorer—Continue what was done with the baby and:

- Remain nearby and attentive.
- Model appropriate behavior.
- Use redirection to stop unacceptable behavior, offering concrete alternatives.
- Recognize the child's feelings with language.
- Appreciate and encourage pro-social behavior.
- Give children words to express emotions.
- Be consistent, yet flexible according to the child's age and temperament.

The individual—Continue what was done with the explorer and:

- Give clear, simple, consistent, predictable rules and consequences.
- Share concerns firmly about hurtful and other inappropriate behaviors.

- Offer reasonable choices when choice is appropriate, and respect preferences.
- Help children make connections between behaviors and consequences.
- Focus on the inappropriate part of the behavior and keep it separate from the appropriate aspects of the behavior.
- Make clear that it is the behavior, not the child, that is unacceptable.
- Point out empathy and caring.

Older children can also benefit from the establishment of a simple set of rules for behavior that are consistently enforced—what Magda Gerber calls "house rules."

The creation of these rules is simple. How to carry them out is the tricky part. All staff members and families should have a conversation about behaviors that will never be allowed in the group: those that are inappropriate but bound to occur and behaviors that teachers want to see. Teachers can then develop lists of these behaviors under three categories: acceptable, inappropriate, and inacceptable. How teachers will relate to these lists is key and follows the lines of an old Johnny Mercer song:

Accentuate the positive
Eliminate the negative
Latch on to the affirmative
Don't mess with Mr. In-between

Encourage appropriate behaviors by paying attention to them. Point out when children behave appropriately, smiling and praising them. Agree as a team as to how you will respond (what actions you all will consistently take) to those behaviors that you have deemed unacceptable and discipline the children for those behaviors, remembering the definition of discipline. For those behaviors that are in the middle—the inappropriate behaviors—do not spend much energy on them; they continue to socialize and guide children but do not nag, discipline, or make a fuss.

After about a month of consistently following this approach, you will find that the positive behaviors will increase, the inappropriate behaviors will start to diminish, and the unacceptable behaviors will become well known to the children as the law of the group. Some children may even start turning in others. However, things will probably become more disruptive at first as children learn the new system. Sticking with a plan is necessary, and this will not happen if your team lacks consistency in implementation or if the program is of such poor quality that the children are either fearful or bored for much of the day. But in normal child care environments, these house rules work wonders. They create a lawful environment for the group and put children at ease. The chart below presents a sample list to consider. The number of unacceptable behaviors should be kept to three or four so that children will not be disciplined for too many things. Above all, it is important to remember, as the song says, to "accentuate the positive."

Individualized Interventions for Disruptive Behavior

The goals are set. The philosophy of guidance is sufficiently clear. The environments are set up, policies and practices have been evaluated, and "house rules" have been established for the older children. Even with these pieces in place, a small number of children will need additional attention. The final piece of the plan for handling issues of socialization is dealing with specific behavior problems. For those issues, the child care team has to plan individual interventions, sometimes having to take unique actions. Here are some things to consider for an intervention.

Behavior-Management Chart for Children Ages 18 Months and Older

Acceptable Behaviors	Inappropriate Behaviors	Unacceptable Behaviors
Persistent	Messy	Physical aggression (hitting, biting, kicking, or hurting other living things)
Curious	Loud	
Works well with others	Flits from one thing to another	Destruction of property
Asks for help		Cursing
Looks at books	Runs	
Initiates activities	Climbs	
	Leaves materials out	

Note: The first two columns should include many more behaviors. Teachers:

1. Observe the child for a week, identifying behaviors that fit in each category. They list only a few unacceptable behaviors.
2. Assess how the environment might contribute to some behaviors and modify the environment as needed.
3. Develop a behavior-management plan. They show enthusiasm for acceptable behaviors and respond to inappropriate behaviors as one would treat a twelve-month-old child.
4. Decide the type of discipline to use for unacceptable behaviors and apply that discipline consistently.

Collaborate with the family

It is imperative to contact the home before starting an individualized intervention. Let the family members know what you are planning and that you would like them to be involved. If you do not do this and they find out about the intervention after the fact, you may never be trusted again. Most of the time there are valuable things to be learned from the child's behavior at home. Cooperative strategies that can be used both at home and in the program work best. Try to have early and frequent meetings with family members. Use their input to develop strategies together and share information about their child's behavior and the strategies you propose for dealing with it.

1. **Assign someone, usually the primary caregiver, to shadow the child for a week or two**

   For that intervention to be successful, you need to first do two things simultaneously: provide emotional support and investigate the situation fully. Decide with the other caregivers which member of the team has the best relationship with the child. That caregiver then shadows the child, spending more time close to him or her to pick up information

about the particulars of the situation, the provocations, the times of day when the child is most likely to engage in the behavior of concern, the people the child is with, the activities or areas of the room where this usually happens. Document your observations so that you can refer to them later as you communicate with families or other staff members and plan for individual children.

2. **"Be with" a child who escalates out of control**

   If a child starts to lose control, the "shadower" should come close to let the child know that he or she is there to be relied on and offer help. Sometimes, you may have to physically remove the child from the situation to keep the child from hurting himself, herself, or someone else. Give the message both verbally and physically, while holding the child, that you will provide the external regulation necessary and that you are there to help the child feel safe.

3. **Provide the child with opportunities to practice self-regulation**

   After an incident has occurred, give the child a chance to have success in accomplishing self-regulation. Try to" stack the deck" for success by setting up a similar experience to the one in which the incident took place. Try a time of day when the child normally has more energy, with children who are less difficult to deal with, or in an area of the room where the child enjoys playing and feels comfortable. Then let the child engage in the experience with your help. Depending on the situation and the child, you can provide support and scaffolds such as using language to help the child recognize and evaluate his or her emotional responses, provide feedback and interpretations (e.g., "he's just coming over to get a truck; he isn't going to take your car"). Finally, acknowledge positive behavior.

4. Maintain predictability

Predictability is both social (*people I know will be there for me*) and spatial (*I know where to find the puzzles and where I can ride the tricycle*). Predictability avoids both chaos and rigidity. For toddlers, predictability involves rituals and rhythms throughout the day that follow sequences (nap, snack, play, then mommy comes) rather than the clock. Create a spatial structure to the environment rather than a time structure for daily activities. Also provide consistency in rules, regulations, and relationships.

5. Prepare child for transitions

Often children exhibiting behavior problems have particular difficulty with transitions. For those children, it is important to make them aware of transitions before they happen. For example, prepare the child by telling him or her, "We will be finishing lunch in just a couple minutes and I will come over and help you move your plate and utensils to the sink." Sometimes you can make an agreement with the child that you will privately let him or her know ahead of time when a transition is about to take place.

6. Overstate social signals (facial expression, vocal tone, gestures, affect) and support understanding of your requests by breaking them into discrete parts.

Sometimes children with behavior issues do not get the messages that

the other children get. You will know this child if you are constantly saying something like this: "I told him a hundred times and he doesn't do what I want." You need to wonder if this child is actually registering your message. Often this child (and the child having troubles with transitions) is so absorbed in the here and now that he misses the subtle cues around him and general messages to the group. Try to be very obvious with your gestures and facial expressions and tone of voice. Dramatize the message. Sometimes you will see a teacher bending down and actually looking right into the eyes of a child to make sure that the child gets the message. But remember that no technique works for everyone. That level of closeness could overwhelm the child whose temperament or family history makes eye-to-eye contact uncomfortable. As with all the other tips, you will always need to discover what works for each child.

7. Provide increased physical and psychological structure

Sometimes children act aggressively when they read situations differently from everyone else. They may come to a situation anxious, angry, or afraid. The hitter, the biter, the pusher may not always, in their minds, be the aggressor or the transgressor. With those children, it is important to create situations for them that keep their anxiety, anger or fear to a minimum. Your presence can be used as an emotional resource. Sometimes you can sit with this child and the one he or she is having trouble with and facilitate the play while you are present. Another time you may be able to share the house rules with the child as you see some trouble developing rather than let things escalate.

8. Attend closely to a child's verbal and nonverbal cues

With children under three years of age, many of the cues they give are nonverbal. Some caregivers look like magicians because they jump into a situation just before it explodes. Often if you observe those

teachers, you will see that they pick up nonverbal cues that indicate what the child will do. As you shadow, you will listen to and watch the child more closely than usual and you will become more skilled at knowing when and how to intervene before a provocative event instead of after it happens.

9. Provide verbal feedback to a child with reference to feelings and behaviors

Sometimes children need help with finding an outlet for their emotions. Your words can provide a scaffold the child can use to move from actions to words. "Wow, it looks like you're really happy." From time to time, ask questions about the child's feelings. "Are you frustrated? I can't tell." "Keesha, are you getting tired or are you sad? It is better to find out the child's feelings by asking a question than to tell a child what she is feeling, for you may be wrong. More important, by asking the child to reflect, you help the child to practice the labeling of feelings.

10. Provide numerous ways for the child to express affect (e.g., symbolic and motor play: reading relevant stories, and so on)

Fantasy play, water play, making up stories, having the child react to stories he or she read—all can be helpful in having the child express affect that might be hidden. You can learn a lot about young children in the fantasy corner. This type of play is often a release for a child exhibiting fear, anger, and even more-than-usual problems with self-regulation.

11. Debrief with each other, at the end of the day, and with the child's family often regarding what worked and did not work with the child

Individual interventions need time for planning and replanning. This type of work can be exhausting to a teacher. Program directors should provide time for debriefing and sometimes substitutes to be in the program while the teachers meet. Sometimes the teacher not doing the shadowing can come to feel that she has to take care of the rest of the classroom. Sometimes the teacher who is doing the shadowing may feel frustrated because she does not seem to think she is making any progress. When teachers think that they might be spinning their wheels, it is wise to bring in a mental health consultant to facilitate the work of the team. Having an ongoing relationship with early childhood mental health specialists can be immensely helpful. They can assist you to reflect on your practices, give you a pair of fresh eyes from which to view the child's behavior, and offer intervention strategies.

Conclusion

Infants depend on adults for many things. One of the most important is learning how to pursue their needs, interests, and desires while considering the needs, interests, and desires of others. This is learned in the early months through interaction with and observation of their caregivers. As they get older, young children look even closer at those who care for them to see how this is done. *When and how can I assert myself? When does my curiosity boil over into destruction of property? When do my initiations*

interfere with the initiations of others? What kinds of emotions are appropriate to express and how loudly can I express them? Children gradually learn answers to these and hundreds of other questions, through day-to-day interaction with those who care for them. As they move out of the infancy period, they slowly incorporate what they have seen and learned into their treatment of others.

But how do you know what to do and what to say to the many different children who come through your care? Well the answer is: "It depends," and it depends on many, many things.

As this chapter has shown, to start with, it depends on you and your beliefs about babies. What you believe about their capacities, drives, needs, and motives influences the goals you will set for them and the ways you will treat them. It depends on the child's developmental equipment. We need to treat similar behaviors differently as the child develops. It depends on the environments set up and the policies and practices instituted. And finally when children present behavior problems, it depends on your skills at investigating what is really happening for that child, your ability to individualize a strategy to pursue to help the child and the relationship you have built or build with the child that you both can rely upon.

Appropriate socialization, guidance, and discipline for children under three are not about knowing how to deal with issues like biting, hitting, or screaming but rather how to deal with children. It is by finding out how they are operating at a particular time in their life under what circumstances and then using that knowledge to support their future development.

References

Brazelton, T. B. 1998. "How to Help Parents of Young Children: The Touchpoints Model." *Clinical Child Psychology and Psychiatry. Special Issue: Parenting* 3(3): 481–83.

Brazelton, T. B., and J. D. Sparrow. 2006. *Touchpoints: Your Child's Emotional and Behavioral Development—Birth to 3.* Cambridge, MA: Da Capo Press.

California Department of Education and WestEd Center for Child & Family Studies. 2009. *California Infant/ Toddler Learning and Development Foundations.* Sacramento: California Department of Education.

Cost, Quality & Child Outcomes Study Team. 1995. *Cost, Quality and Child Outcomes in Child Care Centers: Executive Summary.* Denver: University of Colorado, Economics Department.

Denham, S. A. 1998. *Emotional Development in Young Children.* New York: The Guilford Press.

Fox, N. A., and S. D. Calkins. 2003. "The Development of Self-Control of Emotion: Intrinsic and Extrinsic Influences." *Motivation and Emotion* 27(1): 7–26.

Fraiberg, S. H. 1959. *The Magic Years.* New York: Fireside.

Greven, P. 1988. *The Protestant Temperament: Patterns of Child-Rearing, Religious Experience, and the Self in Early America.* Chicago: University of Chicago Press.

Klages, M. "Lectures on Jacques Lacan." http://www.colorado.edu/English/courses/ENGL2012Klages/lacan.html

Knox, J., and J. Wright. 1977. "A Letter from the Vatican: March 31, 1977, First Penance, First Communion."

Lewis, M., S. M. Alessandri, and M. W. Sullivan. 1992. "Differences in Shame and Pride as a Function of Children's Gender and Task Difficulty." *Child Development* 63(3): 630–38.

Locke, John. 1690. *An Essay Concerning Human Understanding.* 38th ed. London: William Tegg.

National Research Council and Institute of Medicine. 2000. *From Neurons to Neighborhoods: The Science of Early Child Development.* Edited by J. P. Shonkoff and D. A. Phillips. Washington, DC: National Academy Press.

NICHD Early Child Care Research Network. 1996. "Characteristics of Infant Child Care: Factors Contributing to Positive Caregiving." *Early Childhood Research Quarterly* 11: 269–306.

Scaramella, L. V., and L. D. Leve. 2004. "Clarifying Parent-Child Reciprocities During Early Childhood: The Early Childhood Coercion Model." *Clinical Child and Family Psychology Review* 7(2): 89–107.

Silber, K. 1965. *Pestalozzi: The Man and His Work.* 2nd ed. London: Routledge and Kegan Paul.

Suizzo, M., W. Chen, C. Cheng, A. S. Liang, H. Contreras, D. Zanger, and C. Robinson. 2008. "Parental Beliefs About Young Children's Socialization Across US Ethnic Groups: Coexistence of Independence and Interdependence." *Early Child Development and Care* 178(5): 467–86.

Section Four:
Recent Research on Key Topics

Introduction

*I*n this section, Ross A. Thompson, Janet E. Thompson, and Julia Luckenbill discuss the contributions of recent brain development studies to our understanding of early social relationships, temperament, and self-regulation in infants and toddlers. The authors summarize research findings that show how children's early social understanding develops through experiences in relationships. They also explore how caring, nurturing adults can support infants' emerging social understanding and help them form emotionally secure attachments. Through examples from their own work, the authors illustrate how infant care teachers can support children's temperamental individuality and guide the development of self-regulation in infants and toddlers.

Ross A. Thompson, Ph.D., is a professor of psychology at the University of California, Davis (UC Davis). Dr. Thompson's work focuses on early personality and socioemotional development in the context of close relationships, an interest that contributes to the cross-disciplinary field of developmental relational science. This interest takes his work in two directions. First, his research explores the influence of relational processes on emotional growth, conscience development, emotion regulation, and self-understanding. Recent studies have examined, for example, how the content and structure of early parent–child discourse shapes young children's developing representations of emotion, morality, and self. Second, he has worked on the applications of developmental relational science to

public-policy problems concerning children and families, such as divorce and child custody, child maltreatment, grandparent visitation rights, and research ethics.

Janet E. Thompson, M.A., is the director of the Early Childhood Laboratory School at the UC Davis Center for Child and Family Studies, a demonstration program that models a play-based approach to early learning. She earned her M.A. in early childhood education at the University of Michigan and has taught preschool and kindergarten, as well as courses for parents, teachers, and child development students. Her interests include nature education for young children, play-based preschool curriculum development, and the social and emotional aspects of school readiness.

Julia Luckenbill, M.A., is the program coordinator for the infant and toddler components of the Early Childhood Laboratory School at the UC Davis Center for Child and Family Studies. She earned her M.A. in education at Mills College, Oakland, and has directed several preschool programs in California. In addition to her classroom and lecture responsibilities at the center, she gives presentations on a range of child development topics for parents, teachers, and students and is a certified PITC trainer in modules 1–5. Her interests include the use of puppetry to support social and emotional skills, integrating the Reggio Emilia philosophy into schools in the United States, documenting children's learning through photography, and exploring gardens with infants and toddlers.

The Developing Brain and Its Importance to Relationships, Temperament, and Self-regulation

Ross A. Thompson, Janet E. Thompson, and Julia Luckenbill

Caregivers have several lenses that, like magnifying glasses, enable them to view more clearly the development of young children. Our past experience with infants and toddlers focuses our attention on their changing needs. The guidance of more knowledgeable teachers sharpens our awareness of how to contribute to healthy growth. For some, being a parent deepens everyday interactions with young children.

In recent years, another lens has contributed to our understanding of early development. Brain-development research has added new insight to the early growth of the mind and the importance of caregiving influences. We have learned that conversing, reading, and sensitively responding to infants and toddlers strengthen brain connections that provide a basis for lifelong learning. Brain development studies also provide new insights into social and emotional growth. The "scientist in the crib" is revealed by developmental neuroscience to also be a socially insightful, emotionally animated human partner.

What do current studies of brain development contribute to our understanding of early social relationships, temperament, and self-regulation? The purpose of this essay is to profile what we have learned, and what it means for caregivers of in-fants and toddlers. To illustrate the latter, we include examples of caregivers and young children that highlight the interactive strategies we describe.

Relationships and Social Understanding

One of the amazing discoveries yielded by developmental brain research is that beneath the apparently casual play of a young baby is a powerful mind at work. This mind is rapidly expanding in the early years as neurons connect, form networks, and build the architecture of the brain. As a result, infants are learning the sounds of language, cause and effect,

basic concepts, and even simple number reasoning in the early months of life (Gopnik, Meltzoff, and Kuhl 2000).

But the same powerful mind also contributes to early social and emotional understanding (Thompson and Lagattuta 2006). For example, during the first six months of life, babies begin to:

- experience and express joy, interest, sadness, anger, fear, and other emotions;
- identify differences between an adult's facial expressions of sadness, anger, and joy, and understand the emotional meaning of different vocal intonations (such as a warm, melodic tone versus a harsh, angry tone);
- feel resonantly with another's emotional expressions, such as responding with happiness to a caregiver's expressions of joy, or responding to an adult's anger expressions with distress;

- participate in face-to-face play with their caregivers, involving the back-and-forth volleying of social signals (such as eye contact, smiling, and vocalizing) and responding to the social initiatives of the partner;
- differentiate the characteristics of familiar and unfamiliar people;
- develop emotional attachments to the people they see regularly.

By the end of the first year, infants use the emotional expressions of an adult to guide their interpretation of uncertain situations. A one-year-old looks to the mother, for example, after a friendly stranger has greeted her. If mother looks reassuring, the baby is more likely to socialize with the stranger than if mother looks concerned or worried. In addition, the baby will attract mother's attention to the stranger if mother happens to be looking away, as if knowing that the mother's emotional expressions are uninformative if she is not looking at the stranger as well.

By the middle of the second year, toddlers understand that people act according to their desires and feelings, and that people's desires differ. An eighteen-month-old gives broccoli rather than crackers to an adult for a snack after the adult has clearly shown a preference for eating broccoli—even though the toddler prefers the crackers (Repacholi and Gopnik 1997).

These accomplishments reveal that the young child is learning something important about other people. *A person's internal state— feelings, desires, intentions, thoughts, and beliefs— affects his behavior.* Toddlers understand the importance of people's feelings and desires and, as preschoolers, they will learn more about the influence of thoughts and beliefs. Their dawning awareness that these internal states affect a person's outward behavior motivates their interest in learning more about the feelings, desires, goals, and intentions that cause people to act as they do.

Thus the same rapidly developing brain that is the basis for early achievements in language, concepts, and problem-solving is also the foundation for remarkable advances in social understanding and emotional responding. This new lens on early development is causing scientists and practitioners to revise their earlier beliefs about social and emotional development, just as it is revising understanding of early cognitive growth.

We do not think of young children as egocentric, for example (Thompson 2008a). It is clear that they are far too insightful about other people's feelings, desires, and intentions—and how those feelings and so forth differ from their own—for this label to apply. Although infants and toddlers are often confused about *what* other people feel, think, and intend, young children strive to make sense of what is going on in other people's minds because they know it is important to understanding why they act as they do.

Nurturing Social Understanding in Infants and Toddlers

These discoveries are important for how caregivers communicate and connect with young children. Even though their actions may not show it, infants and toddlers take in much more of the social world than we often expect. They are sensitive to the emotions of adults and other children, often looking for explanations of why another child is crying or an adult seems upset. Our words can help them begin to understand the causes of other people's feelings and, in some instances, the reasons for their own emotions. Our words can also help young children

become more emotionally perceptive: saying "it hurt Jamal when you hit him" can focus the child's attention on a consequence of his action that might have been overlooked.

> *Brian, eighteen months old, watches another child. His caregiver says, in a calm voice, "Brian, you hear Jamal crying. He's sad because he fell down. His teacher is holding him and helping him feel better. I wonder if hearing him cry makes you feel sad, too? Would you like me to hold you?"*

At times, young children are living with families in emotional turmoil. A mother is depressed, a father unemployed and angry, and older siblings are upset and resentful. Those emotions are felt deeply by an infant or toddler. When this family emotional climate endures, it begins to affect areas of the brain related to emotions and emotion management, and young children may begin to withdraw and act in a depressed manner themselves (Field and Diego 2008). Sometimes the emotional problems of a young child are the first signs that a family is in difficulty and that an infant or toddler is at emotional risk.

Our responsiveness to a baby's signals also contributes to his social understanding. An infant grunts and leans toward an out-of-reach snack, then looks to the caregiver to see if she is watching and gets the idea. When the adult moves the snack closer, the baby's experiment is confirmed. *I can change her mind!* The baby knows that his desires and goals can alter another's intentions—one person's mental state can affect another's. Every act of sensitive social understanding is, in a sense, a meeting of minds. And for the infant and toddler, these are the foundations of social understanding.

> *Joey (twenty-three months) was seated in the block area. His caregiver, Janet, walked over. "Joey, it's time to wash hands!" she announced. She extended her hand toward him. "Carry Joey?" he asked, extending his arms. Janet repeated his request: "You want me to carry you?" Joey nodded. Janet bent down and lifted him to her hip, carrying him to the sink.*

Talking to young children about their own internal experiences is also important to their self-understanding. When a caregiver uses words to identify a toddler's feelings of sadness and can talk about why the child is feeling this way (e.g., mommy just left for work), it helps young children understand the connections between their internal experience and its causes. This also contributes to social understanding.

> *A caregiver observes Ruth (twenty months): "Ruth, I see you climbed the stairs all by yourself! You look so proud!"*

What does this responsiveness require of a caregiver? It requires *mind-mindedness*. This is the term that researchers give to an adult's awareness of the mental life of a baby. An infant's actions are guided by the baby's goals, intentions, desires, feelings, and other aspects of a rich internal life (Meins et al. 2002). Our mind-mindedness when interacting with a young child enables us to be sensitively responsive to the child's internal experience. In becoming attuned to the child's internal world, we also help the child begin to comprehend the internal states of other people.

> *Maria (fourteen months) and Martin (eleven months) were seated side by side next to a pile of dog pictures. Maria had pulled all the pictures off the wall and was holding them. Martin extended his arms and gripped one, pulling it from Maria. Emily, the teacher, said, "Maria and Martin, it looks like you both want that dog." Both infants continued tugging the picture. Emily held onto the picture. "I can see that you both look pretty upset," Emily continued. Martin tugged the picture again, and it slipped from Maria's fingers. He lifted it to his face. Maria frowned. Emily said, "Oh, it looks like Martin is holding it right now. Maria, you look sad. We can wait for it or find another one." Maria glanced at the floor and found another dog picture. She lifted it up. "You found more!" exclaimed Emily. "Now you each have a dog!"*

Attachment

These brain-based achievements in early social and emotional understanding are the basis for the development of secure attachment relationships. As infants learn about the characteristics and responsiveness of their caregivers, their emotional security becomes organized around these people. At home and in child care, young children turn to trusted attachment figures, particularly in situations when children are alarmed, uncertain, or

distressed and require the emotional support of these adults to manage their feelings. Even during periods of exuberant play or quiet exploration, the availability of these adults provides a "secure base" for infants and toddlers to be confident that if help is needed, their attachment figure will be there.

A caregiver's sensitive responsiveness is the most important determinant of whether a child's attachment will be secure or insecure (Thompson 2001). Sensitive responsiveness includes being attentive to the child's signals and following the child's lead in interaction. It involves responding promptly and appropriately, especially when young children need emotional support. Sensitive responsiveness involves an emotional connection with the child that enables a caregiver to share moments of joy and distress. It incorporates the mind-mindedness mentioned earlier because it is attuned to the internal feelings, desires, intentions, and goals that motivate a child's behavior.

A secure attachment relationship at home or in child care is important for several reasons:

- Security provides confidence for infants and toddlers to explore the world and make discoveries for themselves within the protective orbit of the caregiver's presence.
- Security contributes to the development of social skills and social understanding that enable young children to relate better to other people.
- Security enables young children to view themselves more positively, especially as being loved and lovable.

A secure attachment is also important for managing stressful experiences. At home and in child care, young children naturally encounter situations that are upsetting or frightening, and research shows that stress hormones are lower when children are in the company of adults with whom they are securely attached (National Scientific Council on the Developing Child 2005). This is important because the developing brain can potentially be harmed by persistent high levels of stress hormones, which can occur when children are caught up in the upheaval resulting from chronic, overwhelming, or unpredictable stress. In such circumstances, secure relationships buffer the stress system and protect the developing brain from potentially hazardous influences.

Developing Secure Attachment Relationships in Child Care

Mothers and fathers respond sensitively at home to nurture secure relationships with their infants or toddlers. Caregivers in child care can recognize and affirm the importance of these attachments. When caregivers talk about a child's mother

or father, help parents during transitions with the child at the beginning and end of the day, and encourage children to bring photos of their parents and transition objects to help them through the day, all these activities provide a bridge between attachment relationships at home and children's experience in child care.

> *Brian (eighteen months) was new to the Infant Room. He toddled over to the family photo board. He pulled off his photo and gazed at it. His lower lip trembled. Emily, his caregiver, walked over and knelt beside him. "Brian, you look so sad. I see that you are looking at Mama and Daddy. Mama will come back at circle time. She always comes back for you." Brian extended his arms to Emily. "I can give you a hug," she said, "and I can hold you and keep you safe at school."*

In child care, infants and toddlers encounter frequent challenges and sometimes bring stress with them from home or elsewhere. Children of all ages have more difficulty learning when they are stressed and upset. Therefore secure relationships with child care teachers are important for creating safe, supportive emotional environments that buffer the stresses that young children encounter.

Caregivers can help to create secure attachments with infants and toddlers when they become attuned to the internal experience of the children in their care and avoid being preoccupied by the "tasks" of providing care. As described in Ronald Lally's article, this can occur through the three-step responsive process of:

- *watching* the young child's behavior with empathic attention to the child's experience;
- *asking* how one might act in a manner that enables the child's goals to be achieved;
- *adapting* one's actions according to a sensitive reading of the child's response to them.

This responsiveness becomes more natural as caregivers become more familiar with the children in their care. It may be particularly important for the children who have selected you as the adult to whom they turn for comforting, help, or sharing the excitement of discovery. It is important for infants and toddlers to have a special teacher with whom they create a primary caregiving relationship of security and support. The young child organizes his emotional experience in child care around the teacher, and it is this secure attachment that is most important.

> *Maria (fourteen months) was standing on the climbing stairs in the climbing area. Her lips were pursed, and her eyes scanned the room as she searched for her caregiver, Soo Yung. When the two made eye contact, Maria patted her chest and grinned. Soo Yung also grinned and said, "I see you, Maria. You climbed the stairs!" Maria stepped down the stairs, toddled over to Soo Yung, and gave her a huge hug, smiling all the time. Then she toddled back to the stairs, ducked down, popped up, and repeated the process again.*

The relationship between a young child and the special teacher who has become a primary caregiver is important to the adult as well. Caregivers who spend more time with a particular child are more likely to be capable of sensitively reading the child's cues and understand the meaning of what the child says. Together, the adult and young child are more likely to develop shared ways of communicating, understanding, and comforting. Thus, special relationships with a primary caregiver are important to the development of secure attachments in child care.

Temperament

Developing relationships means recognizing the individuality of each person. Babies are unique from birth. They differ in how active they are, how readily they express emotion, how easily they adapt to new situations, their sociability, and in many other ways. Research on early brain development shows that these broad variations in temperament are based in brain systems that develop significantly in the early years of life. As a result, temperament also develops in infants and toddlers.

In her article, Stella Chess profiles the temperament traits that caregivers use to understand the young children in their care. They include activity level, biological rhythmicity, approach/withdrawal, adaptability, quality of mood, intensity of reactions, sensitivity threshold, distractibility, and persistence/attention span. Each individual trait—and the patterns of traits that characterize the "easy," "difficult," and "slow-to-warm-up" children—help to describe the unique and emergent personality of the child.

In a broader sense, temperament can be described in two dimensions (Rothbart 2004):

- *Reactivity* refers to individual differences in the arousability of the child: how easily the child is moved to action. It includes temperament traits, such as activity level, intensity of reactions, and the emotional qualities of temperament.
- *Self-regulation* refers to individual differences in managing these reactive tendencies. It includes temperament traits such as approach/withdrawal, persistence/attention span, adaptability, and temperamental qualities associated with emotional self-control (such as soothability).

These two dimensions of temperament are associated with brain systems that govern reactivity and self-regulation from birth. Concerning reactivity, certain brain and hormonal systems related to emotion and stress enable newborns to become highly aroused. For this reason, it is easy to see individual differences in the reactivity of young infants. Concerning self-regulation, however, the brain systems that enable infants to manage their arousal and calm down take a longer time to mature. Some temperament characteristics emerge, therefore, as these brain systems mature over time.

Temperament is also affected by experience. Young children who are frequently in difficult and stressful situations, for example, may become more irritable and reactive and less capable of self-

regulation than other children. They react this way because of the influence of stress hormones on the brain systems governing temperament. Because close, secure attachments help to buffer stress, caregiving relationships are especially important for creating a supportive, protective context in which temperament and personality can develop in a healthy manner.

Responding to Temperamental Individuality in Child Care

As in any relationship, appreciating the partner's individuality is important to mutual understanding. This principle is true as caregivers are developing relationships with infants and toddlers. It may be helpful for caregivers to think of the temperaments of children in their care as individual differences in reactivity and self-regulation. *Watching* young children with these differences in mind can help adults *ask* how to respond to each child in a manner that *adapts* to each child's temperamental profile.

- A toddler who is typically emotionally reactive, for example, may need support in expressing strong emotions constructively, such as by seeking the assistance of an adult to solve the problem rather than lashing out with hitting or biting.
- A baby whose self-regulatory tendencies include withdrawing from new experiences, perhaps after a period of watching and indecision, may benefit from a caregiver who can provide a more gradual introduction to a new food or toy. A patient adult may also recognize that an initial rejection does not necessarily predict this young child's later response.
- A young child whose low reactivity includes a preference for low activity may risk being left behind by other children unless a caregiver can help this child find others with a similar preference to engage in quiet play.
- A toddler whose impulsivity reflects low self-regulatory capacities may benefit from a caregiver who provides reminders of the need to respect other children's activities and preferences. However, as seen on the next page, the adult must also recognize young children's limitations in self-control.

Adults can create lifestyles that reflect their personalities and temperaments. They can choose rock-climbing expeditions, membership in book groups, meditation, or dance clubs based on their self-aware characteristics and preferences. When adults are aware of their own temperamental qualities, it can help them understand how they tend to respond to children's temperaments. A caregiver who enjoys vigorous activity may participate more easily in active play with children who share that quality—but may have to make special efforts to enjoy quieter interaction with other children who are more temperamentally quiet and reserved.

Infants and toddlers, however, cannot create lifestyles that reflect their personalities and preferences. They need caregivers who create environments that respect the children's unique temperamental qualities.

This may seem like an impossible challenge when a caregiver is with a group of several children with uniquely different temperaments. How can an adult individualize the experience of each child? Careful consideration of the physical environment and the daily routine is one way of doing so. Does the room provide young children with quiet, soft places for solo play as well as large spaces for noisy, active play? Does the daily schedule allow for alternating times of quiet activity alone (or in pairs) with periods of group activity? If so, it provides opportunities for children of different temperaments.

In addition, when caregivers sensitively monitor the group of children in their care, they may change planned activities to better fit the group. If circle time is not proving interesting, it may be time to move to another activity. If children are becoming too highly aroused by group play, it may be a good idea to move to another activity sooner than planned. When caregivers do so, they increase the likelihood that whatever their temperamental profile, the infants and toddlers in their care will find a constructive place in the group.

Supporting Each Child's Individuality in Child Care

Miranda, a new teacher, was frustrated. Jacob (fourteen months) was all over the classroom, climbing on everything and over his peers. Yael (thirteen months) would sit in the Sensory Area all morning, feeling the texture of pain on her hands. When painting time was over, she did not want to move. Stephen (seventeen months) was yelling and pushing over other children, and Rin (sixteen months) did not want to be placed on the ground and away from the teacher. Miranda had attended a workshop on temperament, and she charted her own traits and the traits of the children. She learned that Jacob needed to be active, Yael had low reactivity, Stephen was somewhat feisty, and Rin was fearful. Miranda also realized that her own moderately active and approachable temperament made her a better fit for some of the toddlers than others, and she learned to adapt to them.

- Stephen was typically emotionally reactive and needed support in expressing strong emotions constructively. Miranda learned to stay near him when other infants or toddlers came close, and she talked about what each child was doing and said that she would help him keep his toys. As Stephen grew older, Miranda coached him to say, "No, that's mine." She advised him to "go around your friends; crashing into them hurts."
- Rin, whose self-regulatory tendencies included withdrawing from new experiences, needed Miranda to provide a more gradual introduction to new things. Rin needed a lot of conversation about anything new, and she needed

caregivers to be as predictable as possible. She also needed to be held a long time before she felt comfortable enough to explore.

- Yael's low reactivity included a preference for low activity. She risked being left behind by other children. Miranda realized that another toddler, Desiree, was a good fit for Yael, and invited her to join them in the Sensory Area. To minimize Yael's characteristic distress, Miranda also began giving her reminders about transitions long before each activity started.

- Jacob, whose behavioral impulsivity reflected low self-regulatory capacities, needed Miranda to provide reminders about respecting other children's activities and preferences. He also needed help remembering what was okay to climb on and that his peers did not like him climbing on them. He needed frequent opportunities to join high-activity games, such as pushing carts in the yard.

Self-regulation

One of the common frustrations of parents and practitioners is the limited self-control of young children. Although adults recognize that they cannot expect much self-management from infants and toddlers, their growing reliance on explanations, incentives, and appeals to self-image reveals their hope that young children, as they mature, will get better at controlling their own behavior. At times, this leads to inappropriate expectations. At home, parents may expect that toddlers will share their toys and cooperate when adults ask them to. At child care, the duration of circle-time activities may stretch the endurance of any two-year-old.

Research on early brain development confirms the wisdom of limited expectations for self-control in young children. The areas of the brain that are most important for self-regulation are among the slowest to mature (National Research Council and Institute of Medicine 2000). Indeed, these brain areas—which are also associated with long-term planning and enacting complex activities—continue to

develop into early adulthood. Infants and toddlers are thus taking their baby steps in the long-term growth of self-control. Their abilities to focus their attention for a sustained time, control their impulses and emotions, and regulate their behavior (such as sitting still) are very limited. Because their brains take a long time to fully mature, young children's self-regulation also takes a long time to develop.

Supporting self-regulation and its development. What does this mean for caregivers? Two things.

First, adults must be cautious in their expectations for young children's self-management. They must be particularly careful to distinguish their hopes that toddlers and preschoolers would manage their feelings, impulses, and attention from a realistic understanding that they can actually do so. The problem is not that young children are egocentric. It is apparent that they have a remarkable capacity for social understanding. Rather, the problem is that they lack the cognitive flexibility to spontaneously inhibit their intended activity (whether it is a tantrum or taking another child's toy) in favor of an alternative course. This is a challenge not only to infants and toddlers but also to older children and some adolescents, because the brain areas necessary for inhibition mature slowly.

In addition, young children sometimes have difficulty remembering what to do or what is expected in everyday situations. Limited memory skills can make it easy for them to forget why they started to put away toys (in preparation for snack time) and become easily distracted by another activity (and begin playing with different toys). Memory skills are part of self-regulation, and these take time to mature, too. Caregivers must be patient and realize that young children are not being deliberately uncooperative or intentionally defiant.

Second, caregivers can make it easier for young children to manage their behavior, feelings, impulses, and desires. The schedule of daily activities and organiza-

tion of the classroom make a big difference in bringing self-regulatory challenges down to a level that young children can manage. To create a manageable environment for self-regulation, caregivers can use the three-step process of *watching*, with empathy, how young children manage everyday challenges; *asking* how they can better help children accomplish their goals; and then *adapting* the classroom and behavior accordingly. Caregivers can:

- design a predictable daily routine so young children can anticipate, and plan for, what happens next, and manage their feelings and expectations accordingly.
- create an organized, consistent classroom environment in which young children can find plenty of toys and materials when they need them, know where to go for different activities, and leave activities that are overarousing, upsetting, or uninteresting.
- break down complex activities into smaller parts. If it is time to transition from play to snack time, for example, adults can guide young children through the process (such as putting away toys, washing hands, and sitting down at the table) in separate steps.
- provide memory aids for what to do next. A wall chart with pictures to identify each step of the daily routine, a song to accompany transitional activities (such as cleanup), or a picture-card that a caregiver displays to signify the next activity are examples of helpful memory aids.
- create a quiet space where young children can retreat to resettle themselves when needed—and helping children find that space when they need it.

- pay attention to signs that children are becoming overaroused, bored, or competitive for limited attention or resources—and adjust activities accordingly. Provide a balance of quiet and active periods in the daily routine.
- use words to communicate understanding of what children are feeling, wanting, or struggling with, and they can help children communicate their feelings to other children.
- offer instructions that focus on what young children *should* do rather than on what they should *not* do (because young children have difficulty inhibiting their activity). When intervening with a child engaged in a prohibited activity (such as climbing up the snack table, for example), acknowledge what the child wants to do (e.g., climb) and offer an alternative (e.g., going to the climbing area in the room or outside).

It is also important to recognize that young children differ in their self-regulatory abilities. Teachers need to remember that self-regulation is an important dimension of temperament. Thus some children will easily manage their impulses and focus their attention on activities (such as circle time) that other children of the same age find more challenging. By carefully watching the children in their care, perhaps making notes about the situations that are easy and difficult to manage, teachers can sensitively respond to each child's individuality in self-regulation.

The room buzzes with activity. In the Quiet Area, toddlers Olivia and Aiden "read" to each other "Old MacDonald Had a Farm," pointing at the images and repeating the text they have memorized. In the nearby Science Area, toddlers Alessandro and Benjamin comment on the pet fish and hamsters while toddler Sophia solves a lock box. The Block Area features Emma and Asher building a tall tower with their caregiver. In the Gross Motor Area, toddlers Tito and Logan are jumping off the stairs and onto the mattress, as the teacher sings, "Tito and Logan are jumping, jumping, jumping! Tito and Logan are jumping at their school!" In the Dramatic Play Area, Noah and Jose are sweeping the carpet with small brushes, and in the Sensory Area, Abby is quietly painting her hands purple with a sponge, the purple paint dripping onto the paper.

Although self-regulatory challenges will remain for many years, children's success in self-control relies both on brain maturation and on the caregiver's sensitivity to children. Caregivers can scaffold the everyday experience to make self-regulation more manageable, enabling children to take pride in their abilities to accomplish goals.

Conclusion

Research on early brain development has sharpened the awareness that a young child's relationships, temperament, and self-regulation are based on brain development, which occurs rapidly. The young brain's rapid growth means that infants and toddlers are more socially aware and emotionally sensitive than is commonly believed. And caregivers have opportunities to contribute to young children's understanding of the social world and to their development of emotional attachments. However, the brain areas related to self-regulation are slowly maturing; therefore, caregivers must guard against expecting too much of young children in their management of attention, feelings, and impulses. Brain-development research is also relevant to understanding reactive and self-regulatory features of a child's developing temperament.

There are many practical implications of this knowledge for how caregivers interact with infants and toddlers in child care (see also California Department of Education 2010). Remarkably, when caregivers use knowledge of relationships, temperament, and self-regulation in the care experiences they create for infants and toddlers, as described above, they create experiences that also nurture developing brains. Young children's brains need:

- warm relationships to provide the security necessary for learning and to help buffer the effects of stress
- the support of a predictable daily routine and an organized environment to support immature brain regions that govern self-regulation;
- sensitive care so that temperamental qualities can unfold in a healthy and constructive manner.

A high-quality early learning environment for infants and toddlers is much different from a high-quality learning environment for older children. One reason is the developing brain (Thompson 2008b); it needs learning environments characterized by warm relationships, lots of social interaction, rich language, choices of activities based on curiosity and discovery, and invitations to active learning. When caregivers and teachers use the best practices in early care and learning, they nurture brain development in young children.

References

California Department of Education. 2010. *California Preschool Curriculum Framework,* Vol. 1. Sacramento: California Department of Education.

Field, T., and M. Diego. 2008. "Maternal Depression Effects on Infant Frontal EEG Asymmetry." *International Journal of Neuroscience* 118: 1081–1108.

Gopnik, A., A. N. Meltzoff, and P. K. Kuhl. 2000. *The Scientist in the Crib.* New York: Harper.

Meins, E., C. Fernyhough, R. Wainwright, M. Das Gupta, E. Fradley, and M. Tuckey. 2002. "Maternal Mind-mindedness and Attachment Security as Predictors of Theory of Mind Understanding." *Child Development* 73(6): 1715–26.

National Scientific Council on the Developing Child. 2005. *Excessive Stress Disrupts the Architecture of the Developing Brain.* Working paper no. 3. http://developingchild.harvard.edu/library/reports_and_working_papers/working_papers/wp3. Cambridge, MA: Harvard University.

Repacholi, B. M., and A. Gopnik. 1997. "Early Reasoning About Desires: Evidence from 14- and 18-month-olds." *Developmental Psychology* 33: 12–21.

Rothbart, M. K. 2004. "Temperament and the Pursuit of an Integrated Developmental Psychology." *Merrill-Palmer Quarterly* 50: 492–505.

Rubin, K. H., and H. S. Rossi, eds. 1982. *Peer Relationships and Social Skills in Childhood.* New York: Springer Verlag.

Shonkoff, J. P., and D. A. Phillips, eds. 2000. *From Neurons to Neighborhoods: The Science of Early Childhood Development.* Washington, DC: National Academy Press.

Thompson, R. A. 2001. "Development in the First Years of Life." *The Future of Children* 11(1): 20–33. http://www.princeton.edu/futureofchildren/publications/journals/journal_details/index.xml?journalid=44.

———. 2008a. "The Psychologist in the Baby." *Zero to Three Journal* 28(5): 5–12.

———. 2008b. "Connecting Neurons, Concepts, and People: Brain Development and Its Implications." *NIEER* (National Institute for Early Education Research) *Preschool Policy Brief 17.* http://nieer.org/docs/index.php?DocID=249.

Thompson, R. A., and K. Lagattuta. 2006. "Feeling and Understanding: Early Emotional Development." In *The Blackwell Handbook of Early Childhood Development*, edited by K. H. McCartney and D. Phillips, 317–37.

Appendix
Social-Emotional
Development
Foundations*

*From the *California Infant/Toddler Learning and Development Foundations* (2009)

Social-Emotional Development

Social-emotional development includes the child's experience, expression, and management of emotions and the ability to establish positive and rewarding relationships with others (Cohen and others 2005). It encompasses both intra- and interpersonal processes.

The core features of emotional development include the ability to identify and understand one's own feelings, to accurately read and comprehend emotional states in others, to manage strong emotions and their expression in a constructive manner, to regulate one's own behavior, to develop empathy for others, and to establish and maintain relationships. (National Scientific Council on the Developing Child 2004, 2)

Infants experience, express, and perceive emotions before they fully understand them. In learning to recognize, label, manage, and communicate their emotions and to perceive and attempt to understand the emotions of others, children build skills that connect them with family, peers, teachers, and the community. These growing capacities help young children to become competent in negotiating increasingly complex social interactions, to participate effectively in relationships and group activities, and to reap the benefits of social support crucial to healthy human development and functioning.

Healthy social-emotional development for infants and toddlers unfolds in an interpersonal context, namely that of positive ongoing relationships with familiar, nurturing adults. Young children are particularly attuned to social and emotional stimulation. Even newborns appear to attend more to stimuli that resemble faces (Johnson and others 1991). They also prefer their mothers' voices to the voices of other women (DeCasper and Fifer 1980). Through nurturance, adults support the infants' earliest experiences of emotion regulation (Bronson 2000a; Thompson and Goodvin 2005).

Responsive caregiving supports infants in beginning to regulate their emotions and to develop a sense of predictability, safety, and responsiveness in their social environments. Early relationships are so important to developing infants that research experts have broadly concluded that, in the early years, "nurturing, stable and consistent relationships are the key to healthy growth, development and learning" (National Research Council and Institute of Medicine 2000, 412). In other words, high-quality relationships increase the likelihood of positive outcomes for young children (Shonkoff 2004). Experiences with family members and teachers provide an opportunity for young children to learn about social relationships and emotions through exploration and predictable interactions. Professionals working in child care settings can support the social-emotional development of infants and toddlers in various ways, including interacting directly with young children, communicating with families, arranging the physical space in the care environment, and planning and implementing curriculum.

Brain research indicates that emotion and cognition are profoundly interrelated processes. Specifically, "recent cognitive neuroscience findings suggest that the neural mechanisms underlying emotion regulation may be the same as those underlying cognitive processes" (Bell and Wolfe 2004, 366). Emotion and cognition work together, jointly informing the child's impressions of situations and influencing behavior. Most learning in the early years occurs in the context of emotional supports (National Research Council and Institute of Medicine 2000). "The rich interpenetrations of emotions and cognitions establish the major psychic scripts for each child's life" (Panksepp 2001). Together, emotion and cognition contribute to attentional processes, decision making, and learning (Cacioppo and Berntson 1999). Furthermore, cognitive processes, such as decision making, are affected by emotion (Barrett and others 2007). Brain structures involved in the neural circuitry of cognition influence emotion and vice versa (Barrett and others 2007). Emotions and social behaviors affect the young child's ability to persist in goal-oriented activity, to seek help when it is needed, and to participate in and benefit from relationships.

Young children who exhibit healthy social, emotional, and behavioral adjustment are more likely to have good academic performance in elementary school (Cohen and others 2005; Zero to Three 2004). The sharp distinction between cognition and emotion that has historically been made may be more of an artifact of scholarship than it is representative of the way these processes occur in the brain (Barrett and others 2007). This recent research strengthens the view that early childhood programs support later positive learning outcomes in all domains by maintaining a focus on the promotion of healthy social emotional development (National Scientific Council on the Developing Child 2004; Raver 2002; Shonkoff 2004).

Interactions with Adults

Interactions with adults are a frequent and regular part of infants' daily lives. Infants as young as three months of age have been shown to be able to discriminate between the faces of unfamiliar adults (Barrera and Maurer 1981). The foundations that describe Interactions with Adults and Relationships with Adults are interrelated. They jointly give a picture of healthy social-emotional development that is based in a supportive social environment established by adults. Children develop the ability to both respond to adults and engage with them first through predictable interactions in close relationships with parents or other caring adults at home and outside the home. Children use and build upon the skills learned through close relationships to interact with less familiar adults in their lives. In interacting with adults, children engage in a wide variety of social exchanges such as establishing contact with a relative or engaging in storytelling with an infant care teacher.

Quality in early childhood programs is, in large part, a function of the interactions that take place between the adults and children in those programs. These interactions form the basis for the relationships that are established between teachers and children in the classroom or home and are related to children's developmental status. How teachers interact with children is at the very heart of early childhood education (Kontos and Wilcox-Herzog 1997, 11).

Relationships with Adults

Close relationships with adults who provide consistent nurturance strengthen children's capacity to learn and develop. Moreover, relationships with parents, other family members, caregivers, and teachers provide the key context for infants' social-emotional development. These special relationships influence the infant's emerging sense of self and understanding of others. Infants use relationships with adults in many ways: for reassurance that they are safe, for assistance in alleviating distress, for help with emotion regulation, and for social approval or encouragement. Establishing close relationships with adults is related to children's emotional security, sense of self, and evolving understanding of the world around them. Concepts from the literature on attachment may be applied to early childhood settings, in considering the infant care teacher's role in separations and reunions during the day in care, facilitating the child's exploration, providing comfort, meeting physical needs, modeling positive relationships, and providing support during stressful times (Raikes 1996).

Interactions with Peers

In early infancy children interact with each other using simple behaviors such as looking at or touching another child. Infants' social interactions with peers increase in complexity from engaging in repetitive or routine back-and-forth interactions with peers (for example, rolling a ball back and forth) to engaging in cooperative activities such as building a tower of blocks together or acting out different roles during pretend play. Through interactions with peers, infants explore their interest in others and learn about social behavior/social interaction. Interactions with peers provide the context for social learning and problem solving, including the experience of social exchanges, cooperation, turn-taking, and the demonstration of the beginning of empathy. Social interactions with peers also allow older infants to experiment with different roles in small groups and in different situations such as relating to familiar versus unfamiliar children. As noted, the foundations called Interactions with Adults, Relationships with Adults, Interactions with Peers, and Relationships with Peers are interrelated. Interactions are stepping-stones to relationships. Burk (1996, 285) writes:

> We, as teachers, need to facilitate the development of a psychologically safe environment that promotes positive social interaction. As children interact openly with their peers, they learn more about each other as individuals, and they begin building a history of interactions.

Relationships with Peers

Infants develop close relationships with children they know over a period of time, such as other children in the family child care setting or neighborhood. Relationships with peers provide young children with the opportunity to develop strong social connections. Infants often show a preference for playing and being with friends, as compared with peers with whom they do not have a relationship. Howes' (1983) research suggests that there are distinctive patterns of friendship for the infant, toddler, and preschooler age groups. The three groups vary in the number of friendships, the stability of friendships, and the nature of interaction between friends (for example, the extent to which they involve object exchange or verbal communication).

Identity of Self in Relation to Others

Infants' social-emotional development includes an emerging awareness of self and others. Infants demonstrate this foundation in a number of ways. For example, they can respond to their names, point to their body parts when asked, or name members of their families. Through an emerging understanding of other people in their social environment, children gain an understanding of their roles within their families and communities. They also become aware of their own preferences and characteristics and those of others.

Recognition of Ability

Infants' developing sense of self-efficacy includes an emerging understanding that they can make things happen and that they have particular abilities. Self-efficacy is related to a sense of competency, which has been identified as a basic human need (Connell 1990). The development of children's sense of self-efficacy may be seen in play or exploratory behaviors when they act on an object to produce a result. For example, they pat a musical toy to make sounds come out. Older infants may demonstrate recognition of ability through "I" statements, such as "I did it" or "I'm good at drawing."

Expression of Emotion

Even early in infancy, children express their emotions through facial expressions, vocalizations, and body language. The later ability to use words to express emotions gives young children a valuable tool in gaining the assistance or social support of others (Saarni and others 2006). Temperament may play a role in children's ex-

pression of emotion. Tronick (1989, 112) described how expression of emotion is related to emotion regulation and communication between the mother and infant: "the emotional expressions of the infant and the caretaker function to allow them to mutually regulate their interactions . . . the infant and the adult are participants in an affective communication system."

Both the understanding and expression of emotion are influenced by culture. Cultural factors affect children's growing understanding of the meaning of emotions, the developing knowledge of which situations lead to which emotional outcomes, and their learning about which emotions are appropriate to display in which situations (Thompson and Goodvin 2005). Some cultural groups appear to express certain emotions more often than other cultural groups (Tsai, Levenson, and McCoy 2006). In addition, cultural groups vary by which particular emotions or emotional states they value (Tsai, Knutson, and Fung 2006). One study suggests that cultural differences in exposure to particular emotions through storybooks may contribute to young children's preferences for particular emotional states (for example, excited or calm) (Tsai and others 2007).

Young children's expression of positive and negative emotions may play a significant role in their development of social relationships. Positive emotions appeal to social partners and seem to enable relationships to form, while problematic management or expression of negative emotions leads to difficulty in social relationships (Denham and Weissberg 2004). The use of emotion-related words appears to be associated with how likable preschoolers are considered by their peers. Children who use emotion-related words were found to be better-liked by their classmates (Fabes and others 2001). Infants respond more positively to adult vocalizations that have a positive affective tone (Fernald 1993). Social smiling is a developmental process in which neurophysiology and cognitive, social, and emotional factors play a part, seen as a "reflection and constituent of an interactive relationship" (Messinger and Fogel 2007, 329). It appears likely that the experience of positive emotions is a particularly important contributor to emotional well-being and psychological health (Fredrickson 2000, 2003; Panksepp 2001).

Empathy

During the first three years of life, children begin to develop the capacity to experience the emotional or psychological state of another person (Zahn-Waxler and Radke-Yarrow 1990). The following definitions of empathy are found in the research literature: "knowing what another person is feeling," "feeling what another person is feeling," and "responding compassionately to another's distress" (Levenson and Ruef 1992, 234). The concept of empathy reflects the social nature of emotion, as it links the feelings of two or more people (Levenson and Ruef 1992). Since human life is relationship-based, one vitally important function of empathy over the life span is to strengthen social bonds (Anderson and Keltner 2002). Research has shown a correlation between empathy and prosocial behavior (Eisenberg 2000). In particular, prosocial behaviors, such as helping, sharing, and comforting or showing concern for others, illustrate the development of empathy (Zahn-Waxler and others 1992) and how the experience of empathy is thought to be related to the development of moral behavior (Eisenberg 2000). Adults model prosocial/empathic behaviors for

infants in various ways. For example, those behaviors are modeled through caring interactions with others or through providing nurturance to the infant. Quann and Wien (2006, 28) suggest that one way to support the development of empathy in young children is to create a culture of caring in the early childhood environment: "Helping children understand the feelings of others is an integral aspect of the curriculum of living together. The relationships among teachers, between children and teachers, and among children are fostered with warm and caring interactions."

Emotion Regulation

The developing ability to regulate emotions has received increasing attention in the research literature (Eisenberg, Champion, and Ma 2004). Researchers have generated various definitions of emotion regulation, and debate continues as to the most useful and appropriate way to define this concept (Eisenberg and Spinrad 2004). As a construct, emotion regulation reflects the interrelationship of emotions, cognitions, and behaviors (Bell and Wolfe 2004). Young children's increasing understanding and skill in the use of language is of vital importance in their emotional development, opening new avenues for communicating about and regulating emotions (Campos, Frankel, and Camras 2004) and helping children to negotiate acceptable outcomes to emotionally charged situations in more effective ways. Emotion regulation is influenced by culture and the historical era in which a person lives: cultural variability in regulation processes is significant (Mesquita and Frijda 1992). "Cultures vary in terms of what one is expected to feel, and when, where, and with whom one may express different feelings" (Cheah and Rubin 2003, 3). Adults can provide positive role models of emotion regulation through their behavior and through the verbal and emotional support they offer children in managing their emotions. Responsiveness to infants' signals contributes to the development of emotion regulation. Adults support infants' development of emotion regulation by minimizing exposure to excessive stress, chaotic environments, or over- or understimulation.

Emotion regulation skills are important in part because they play a role in how well children are liked by peers and teachers and how socially competent they are perceived to be (National Scientific Council on the Developing Child 2004). Children's ability to regulate their emotions appropriately can contribute to perceptions of their overall social skills as well as to the extent to which they are liked by peers (Eisenberg and others 1993). Poor emotion regulation can impair children's thinking, thereby compromising their judgment and decision making (National Scientific Council on the Developing Child 2004). At kindergarten entry, children demonstrate broad variability in their ability to self-regulate (National Research Council and Institute of Medicine 2000).

Impulse Control

Children's developing capacity to control impulses helps them adapt to social situations and follow rules. As infants grow, they become increasingly able to exercise voluntary control over behavior such as waiting for needs to be met, inhibiting potentially hurtful behavior, and acting according to social expectations, including safety rules. Group care settings provide many opportunities for children to practice their impulse-control skills. Peer interactions often offer natural opportunities for young children to practice impulse control, as they make progress in learning about cooperative play and sharing. Young children's understanding or lack of understanding of requests made of them may be one factor contributing to their responses (Kaler and Kopp 1990).

Social Understanding

During the infant/toddler years, children begin to develop an understanding of the responses, communication, emotional expression, and actions of other people. This development includes infants' understanding of what to expect from others, how to engage in back-and-forth social interactions, and which social scripts are to be used for which social situations. "At each age, social cognitive understanding contributes to social competence, interpersonal sensitivity, and an awareness of how the self relates to other individuals and groups in a complex social world" (Thompson 2006, 26). Social understanding is particularly important because of the social nature of humans and human life, even in early infancy (Wellman and Lagattuta 2000). Recent research suggests that infants' and toddlers' social understanding is related to how often they experience adult communication about the thoughts and emotions of others (Taumoepeau and Ruffman 2008).

Foundation: Interactions with Adults

The developing ability to respond to and engage with adults

8 months	18 months	36 months
At around eight months of age, children purposefully engage in reciprocal interactions and try to influence the behavior of others. Children may be both interested in and cautious of unfamiliar adults. (7 mos.; Lamb, Bornstein, and Teti 2002, 340) (8 mos.; Meisels and others 2003, 16)	At around 18 months of age, children may participate in routines and games that involve complex back-and-forth interaction and may follow the gaze of the infant care teacher to an object or person. Children may also check with a familiar infant care teacher when uncertain about something or someone. (18 mos.; Meisels and others 2003, 33)	At around 36 months of age, children interact with adults to solve problems or communicate about experiences or ideas. (California Department of Education 2005, 6; Marvin and Britner 1999, 60).
For example, the child may:	**For example, the child may:**	**For example, the child may:**
• Attend to an unfamiliar adult with interest but show wariness or become anxious when that adult comes too close. (5–8 mos.; Parks 2004; Johnstone and Scherer 2000, 222) • Take the infant care teacher's hands and rock forward and backwards as a way of asking her to sing a favorite song. (8 mos.; Gustafson, Green, and West 1979; Kaye and Fogel 1980) • Engage in games such as pat-a-cake and peek-a-boo. (7–9 mos.; Coplan 1993, 3) • Make eye contact with a family member. • Vocalize to get an infant care teacher's attention.	• Move close to the infant care teacher and hold his hand when a visitor enters the classroom but watch the visitor with interest. (18 mos.; Meisels and others 2003) • Bring a familiar object to an adult when asked. (15–18 mos.; Parks 2004) • Allow an unfamiliar adult to get close only after the adult uses an object to bridge the interaction, such as showing interest in a toy that is also interesting to the child. (18 mos.; Meisels and others 2003) • Watch, and then help the infant care teacher as she prepares snack. • Seek reassurance from the infant care teacher when unsure if something is safe. (10–12 mos.; Fogel 2001, 305; Dickstein and Parke 1988; Hirshberg and Svejda 1990)	• Participate in storytelling with the infant care teacher. (30–36 mos.; Parks 2004) • Tell a teacher from the classroom next door about an upcoming birthday party. (36 mos.; Parks 2004) • Help the infant care teacher bring in the wheeled toys from the play yard at the end of the day. • Ask a classroom visitor her name.
Behaviors leading up to the foundation (4 to 7 months)	**Behaviors leading up to the foundation (9 to 17 months)**	**Behaviors leading up to the foundation (19 to 35 months)**
During this period, the child may: • Engage in playful, face-to-face winteractions with an adult, such as taking turns vocalizing and then smiling or laughing. (2–7 mos.; Lamb, Bornstein, and Teti 2002, 375) • Begin to protest separations from significant adults.	During this period, the child may: • Engage in back-and-forth interaction by handing a parent an object, then reaching to receive the object when it is handed back. (9–12 mos.; Lerner and Ciervo 2003) • Show—but not give—a toy to the infant care teacher. (9–12 mos.; Parks 2004)	During this period, the child may: • Practice being a grown-up during pretend play by dressing up or using a play stove. (18–36 mos.; Lerner and Dombro 2000) • Help the infant care teacher clean up after snack by putting snack dishes in the dish bin.

Foundation: Relationships with Adults

The development of close relationships with certain adults who provide consistent nurturance

8 months	18 months	36 months
At around eight months of age, children seek a special relationship with one (or a few) familiar adult(s) by initiating interactions and seeking proximity, especially when distressed. (6–9 mos.; Marvin and Britner 1999, 52)	At around 18 months of age, children feel secure exploring the environment in the presence of important adults with whom they have developed a relationship over an extended period of time. When distressed, children seek to be physically close to these adults. (6–18 mos.; Marvin and Britner 1999, 52; Bowlby 1983)	At around 36 months of age, when exploring the environment, from time to time children reconnect, in a variety of ways, with the adult(s) with whom they have developed a special relationship: through eye contact; facial expressions; shared feelings; or conversations about feelings, shared activities, or plans. When distressed, children may still seek to be physically close to these adults. (By 36 mos.; Marvin and Britner 1999, 57)
For example, the child may:	**For example, the child may:**	**For example, the child may:**
• Seek comfort from the infant care teacher by crying and looking for him. (7 mos.a; Lamb, Bornstein, and Teti 2002, 372) • Cry out or follow after a parent when dropped off at the child care program. (6–9 mos.; Ainsworth1967, 4) • Lift her arms to be picked up by the special infant care teacher. (8 mos.; Meisels and others 2003, 17; Ainsworth 1967, 5) • Crawl toward a parent when startled by a loud noise. (8.5 mos.; Marvin and Britner 1999, 52) • Turn excitedly and raise his arms to greet a family member at pick-up time. (8 mos.; Ainsworth 1967, 5)	• Run in wide circles around the outdoor play area, circling back each time and hug the legs of the infant care teacher before running off again. • Snuggle with the special infant care teacher when feeling tired or grumpy. • Wave at the special infant care teacher from the top of the slide to make sure he is watching. • Follow a parent physically around the room. • Play away from the infant care teacher and then move close to him from time to time to check in. (12 mos.; Davies 2004, 10)	• Feel comfortable playing on the other side of the play yard away from the infant care teacher, but cry to be picked up after falling down. (24–36 mos.; Lamb, Bornstein, and Teti 2002, 376) • Call "Mama!" from across the room while playing with dolls to make sure that the mother is paying attention. (24–36 mos.; Schaffer and Emerson 1964) • Call for a family member and look out the window for him after being dropped off at school. (24–36 mos.; Marvin and Britner 1999, 56) • Communicate, "This is our favorite part" when reading a funny story with the infant care teacher. • Bring the grandmother's favorite book to her and express, "One more?" to see if she will read one more book, even though she has just said, "We're all done reading. Now it's time for nap." (Teti 1999; 18–36 mos.; Marvin and Britner 1999, 59) • Cry and look for the special infant care teacher after falling. • Seek the attention of the special infant care teacher and communicate, "Watch me!" before proudly displaying a new skill.

Chart continues on next page.

Relationships with Adults

Behaviors leading up to the foundation (4 to 7 months)	Behaviors leading up to the foundation (9 to 17 months)	Behaviors leading up to the foundation (19 to 35 months)
During this period, the child may: • Hold on to a parent's sweater when being held. (5 mos.; Marvin and Britner 1999, 51; Ainsworth 1967, 1) • Babble back and forth with the infant care teacher. (3–6 mos.; Caufield 1995) • Be more likely to smile when approached by the infant care teacher than a stranger. (3–6 mos.; Marvin and Britner 1999, 50) • Cry when an unfamiliar adult gets too close. (7 mos.; Bronson 1972)	During this period, the child may: • Cry and ask for a parent after being dropped off in the morning. (9–12 mos.; Lerner and Ciervo 2003) • Look for a smile from the infant care teacher when unsure if something is safe. (10–12 mos.; Fogel 2001, 305; Dickstein and Parke 1988; Hirshberg and Svejda 1990) • Cling to a parent when feeling ill. (10–11 mos.; Marvin and Britner 1999, 52)	During this period, the child may: • Say, "I go to school. Mama goes to work," after being dropped off in the morning. • Gesture for one more hug as a parent is leaving for work.

Foundation: Interactions with Peers

The developing ability to respond to and engage with other children

8 months	18 months	36 months
At around eight months of age, children show interest in familiar and unfamiliar peers. Children may stare at another child, explore another child's face and body, and respond to siblings and older peers. (8 mos.; Meisels and others 2003)	At around 18 months of age, children engage in simple back-and-forth interactions with peers for short periods of time. (Meisels and others 2003, 35)	At around 36 months of age, children engage in simple cooperative play with peers. (36 mos.; Meisels and others 2003 70)
For example, the child may:	**For example, the child may:**	**For example, the child may:**
• Watch other children with interest. (8 mos.; Meisels and others 2003) • Touch the eyes or hair of a peer. (8 mos.; Meisels and others 2003) • Attend to a crying peer with a serious expression. (7 mos.; American Academy of Pediatrics 2004, 212) • Laugh when an older sibling or peer makes a funny face. (8 mos.; Meisels and others 2003)	• Hit another child who takes a toy. (18 mos.; Meisels and others 2003, 35) • Offer a book to another child, perhaps with encouragement from the infant care teacher. (18 mos.; Meisels and others 2003, 35) • Tickle another child, get tickled back, and tickle him again. (18 mos.; Meisels and others 2003, 35) • Engage in reciprocal play, such as run-and-chase or offer-and-receive. (12–13 mos.; Howes 1988, v; 10–12 mos.; Ross and Goldman 1977) • Play ball with a peer by rolling the ball back and forth to each other. (12–15 mos.; Parks 2004; 9–16 mos.; Frankenburg and others 1990)	• Communicate with peers while digging in the sandbox together. (29–36 mos.; Hart and Risley 1999, 124) • Act out different roles with peers, sometimes switching in and out of her role. (By 36 mos.; Segal 2004, 44) • Build a tall tower with one or two other children. (36 mos.; Meisels and others 2003, 70) • Hand a peer a block or piece of railroad track when building.

Chart continues on next page.

Interactions with Peers

Behaviors leading up to the foundation (4 to 7 months)	Behaviors leading up to the foundation (9 to 17 months)	Behaviors leading up to the foundation (19 to 35 months)
During this period, the child may: • Notice other infants and children while sitting on a parent's or infant care teacher's lap. • Cry when hearing another baby cry. (4 mos.; Meisels and others 2003, 10)	During this period, the child may: • Engage in solitary play. (toddler; Segal 2004, 38) • Play a reciprocal game, such as pat-a-cake, with the infant care teacher and a peer. (7–11 mos.; Frankenburg and othres 1990)	During this period, the child may: • Use gestures to communicate a desire to play with a peer. (18–24 mos.; Parks 2004, 123) • Refuse to let a peer have a turn on the swing. (24 mos.; Meisels and others 2003, 45) • Push or bite when another child takes a toy. (24–30 mos.; Parks 2004) • Engage in complementary interactions, such as feeding a stuffed animal that another child is holding or pulling a friend in the wagon. (24–30 mos.; Meisels and others 2003, 57; Howes and Matheson 1992, 967) • Join a group of children who are together in one play space and follow them as they move outside. (30 mos.; Meisels and others 2003, 57)

Foundation: Relationships with Peers

The development of relationships with certain peers through interactions over time

8 months	18 months	36 months
At around eight months of age, children show interest in familiar and unfamiliar children. (8 mos.; Meisels and others 2003, 17)	At around 18 months of age, children prefer to interact with one or two familiar children in the group and usually engage in the same kind of back-and-forth play when interacting with those children. (12–18 mos.; Mueller and Lucas 1975)	At around 36 months of age, children have developed friendships with a small number of children in the group and engage in more complex play with those friends than with other peers.
For example, the child may:	**For example, the child may:**	**For example, the child may:**
• Watch other children with interest. (8 mos.; Meisels and others 2003) • Touch the eyes or hair of a peer. (8 mos.; Meisels and others 2003) • Attend to a crying peer with a serious expression. (7 mos.; American Academy of Pediatrics 2004, 212) • Laugh when an older sibling or peer makes a funny face. (8 mos.; Meisels and others 2003) • Try to get the attention of another child by smiling at him or babbling to him (6–9 mos.; Hay, Pederson, and Nash 1982)	• Play the same kind of game, such as run-and-chase, with the same peer almost every day. (Howes 1987, 259) • Choose to play in the same area as a friend. (Howes 1987, 259)	• Choose to play with a sibling instead of a less familiar child. (24–36 mos.; Dunn 1983, 795) • Exhibit sadness when the favorite friend is not at school one day. (24–36 mos.; Melson and Cohen 1981) • Seek one friend for running games and another for building with blocks. (Howes 1987) • Play "train" with one or two friends for an extended period of time by pretending that one is driving the train and the rest are riding.
Behaviors leading up to the foundation (4 to 7 months)	**Behaviors leading up to the foundation (9 to 17 months)**	**Behaviors leading up to the foundation (19 to 35 months)**
During this period, the child may: • Look at another child who is lying on the blanket nearby. (4 mos.; Meisels and others 2003, 10) • Turn toward the voice of a parent or older sibling. (4 mos.; Meisels and others 2003, 10)	During this period, the child may: • Watch an older sibling play nearby. (12 mos.; Meisels and others 2003, 26) • Bang blocks together next to a child who is doing the same thing. (12 mos.; Meisels and others 2003, 26) • Imitate the simple actions of a peer. (9–12 mos.; Ryalls, Gul, and Ryalls 2000)	During this period, the child may: • Engage in social pretend play with one or two friends; for example, pretend to be a dog while a friend pretends to be the owner. (24–30 mos.; Howes 1987, 261) • Express an interest in playing with a particular child. (13–24 mos.; Howes 1988, 3)

Chart continues on next page.

Foundation: Identity of Self in Relation to Others

The developing concept that the child is an individual operating within social relationships

8 months	18 months	36 months
At around eight months of age, children show clear awareness of being a separate person and of being connected with other people. Children identify others as both distinct from and connected to themselves. (Fogel 2001, 347)	At around 18 months of age, children demonstrate awareness of their characteristics and express themselves as distinct persons with thoughts and feelings. Children also demonstrate expectations of others' behaviors, responses, and characteristics on the basis of previous experiences with them.	At around 36 months of age, children identify their feelings, needs, and interests, and identify themselves and others as members of one or more groups by referring to categories. (24–36 mos.; Fogel 2001, 415; 18–30 mos.)
For example, the child may:	**For example, the child may:**	**For example, the child may:**
• Respond to someone who calls her name. (5–7 mos.; Parks 2004, 94; 9 mo.; Coplan 1993, 2) • Turn toward a familiar person upon hearing his name. (6–8 mos.; Parks 2004, 94; 8 mos.; Meisels and others 2003, 18) • Look at an unfamiliar adult with interest but show wariness or become anxious when that adult comes too close. (5–8 mos.; Parks 2004; Johnstone and Scherer 2000, 222) • Wave arms and kick legs when a parent enters the room. • Cry when the favorite infant care teacher leaves the room. (6–10 mos.; Parks 2004)	• Point to or indicate parts of the body when asked. (15–19 mos.; Parks 2004) • Express thoughts and feelings by saying "no!" (18 mos.; Meisels and others 2003) • Move excitedly when approached by an infant care teacher who usually engages in active play.	• Use pronouns such as I, me, you, we, he, and she. (By 36 mo.; American Academy of Pediatrics 2004, p. 307) • Say own name. (30–33 mos.; Parks 2004, 115) • Begin to make comparisons between self and others; for example, communicate, "_____ is a boy/girl like me." • Name people in the family. • Point to pictures of friends and say their names. • Communicate, "Do it myself!" when the infant care teacher tries to help.

Chart continues on next page.

Identity of Self in Relation to Others

Behaviors leading up to the foundation (4 to 7 months)	Behaviors leading up to the foundation (9 to 17 months)	Behaviors leading up to the foundation (19 to 35 months)
During this period, the child may:	During this period, the child may:	During this period, the child may:
• Use hands to explore different parts of the body. (4 mos.; Kravitz, Goldenberg, and Neyhus 1978)	• Play games such as peek-a-boo or run-and-chase with the infant care teacher. (Stern 1985, 102; 7–11 mos.; Frankenburg and others 1990)	• Recognize his own image in the mirror and understand that it is himself. (Siegel 1999, 35; Lewis and Brooks-Gunn 1979, 56)
• Examine her own hands and a parent's hands. (Scaled score of 9 for 4:06–4:15 mos.;* Bayley 2006, 53)	• Recognize familiar people, such as a neighbor or infant care teacher from another room, in addition to immediate family members. (12–18 mo.; Parks 2004)	• Know the names of familiar people, such as a neighbor. (by end of second year; American Academy of Pediatrics 2004, 270)
• Watch or listen for the infant care teacher to come to meet the child's needs. (Birth–8 mos.; Lerner and Dombro 2000, 42)	• Use names to refer to significant people; for example, "Mama" to refer to the mother and "Papa" to refer to the father. (11–14 mos.; Parks 2004, 109)	• Show understanding of or use words such as you, me, mine, he, she, it, and I. (20–24 mos.; Parks 2004, 96; 20 mos.; Bayley 2006; 18–24 mos.; Lerner and Ciervo 2003; 19 mos.; Hart and Risley 1999, 61; 24–20 mos.; Parks 2004, 113)
		• Use name or other family label (e.g., nickname, birth order, "little sister") when referring to self. (18–24 mo.; Parks 2004; 24 mo.; Lewis and Brooks-Gunn 1979)
		• Claim everything as "mine." (24 mos.; Levine 1983)
		• Point to or indicate self in a photograph. (24 mos.; Lewis and Brooks-Gunn 1979)
		• Proudly show the infant care teacher a new possession. (24–30 mos.; Parks 2004)

Foundation: Recognition of Ability

The developing understanding that the child can take action to influence the environment

8 months	18 months	36 months
At around eight months of age, children understand that they are able to make things happen.	At around 18 months of age, children experiment with different ways of making things happen, persist in trying to do things even when faced with difficulty, and show a sense of satisfaction with what they can do. (McCarty, Clifton, and Collard 1999)	At around 36 months of age, children show an understanding of their own abilities and may refer to those abilities when describing themselves.
For example, the child may:	**For example, the child may:**	**For example, the child may:**
• Pat a musical toy to try to make the music come on again. (5–9 mos.; Parks 2004) • Raise arms to be picked up by the infant care teacher. (6–9 mos.; Fogel 2001, 274) • Initiate a favorite game; for example, hold out a foot to a parent to start a game of "This Little Piggy." (8 mos.; Meisels and others 2003; 6–9 mos.; Fogel 2001, 274) • Gesture at a book and smile with satisfaction after the infant care teacher gets it down from the shelf. (8 mos.; Meisels and others 2003)	• Roll a toy car back and forth on the ground and then push it really hard and let go to see what happens. (18 mos.; McCarty, Clifton, and Collard 1999) • Clap and bounce with joy after making a handprint with paint. (12–18 mos.; Sroufe 1979; Lally and others 1995, 71) • Squeeze a toy in different ways to hear the sounds it makes. (Scaled score of 10 for 13:16–14:15 mos.;* Bayley 2006) • Smile after walking up a steep incline without falling or carrying a bucket full of sand from one place to another without spilling. • Proudly hold up a book hidden in a stack after being asked by the infant care teacher to find it.	• Communicate, "I take care of the bunny" after helping to feed the class rabbit. (18–36 mos.; Lally and others 1995, 71) • Finish painting a picture and hold it up to show a family member. • Complete a difficult puzzle for the first time and clap or express, "I'm good at puzzles."

Chart continues on next page.

Recognition of Ability

Behaviors leading up to the foundation (4 to 7 months)	Behaviors leading up to the foundation (9 to 17 months)	Behaviors leading up to the foundation (19 to 35 months)
During this period, the child may: • Try again and again to roll over, even though not yet able to roll completely over. • Grasp, suck, or look at a teething ring. (Before 8 mos. of age; Fogel 2001, 218) • Shake a toy, hear it make noise, and shake it again. • Stop crying upon seeing the infant care teacher approach with a bottle.	During this period, the child may: • Drop a blanket over the side of the crib and wait for the infant care teacher to pick it up. (12 mos.; Meisels and others 2003) • Drop a toy truck in the water table and blink in anticipation of the big splash. (12 mos.; Meisels and others 2003) • Look over a shoulder, smile at the mother, and giggle in a playful way while crawling past her, to entice her to play a game of run-and-chase. (10–14 mos.; Bayley 2006) • Turn light switch on and off repeatedly.	During this period, the child may: • Insist on zipping up a jacket when the infant care teacher tries to help. (20–28 mos.; Hart and Risley 1999, 62; 24 mos.; Hart and Risley 1999, 122 and 129; 20–36 mos.; Bates 1990; Bullock and Lutkenhaus 1988, 1990; Stipek, Gralinski, and Kopp 1990) • Point to a stack of blocks he has made and express, "look" to the infant care teacher. (28 mos.; Hart and Risley 1999, 96) • Communicate, "I doing this," "I don't do this, " "I can do this," or "I did this." (25 mos.; Hart and Risley 1999, 121; Dunn, 1987; Stipek, Gralinski, and Kopp 1990) • Say, "I climb high" when telling the infant care teacher about what happened during outside play time, then run outside to show him how. (30 mos.; Meisels and others 2003)

Foundation: Expression of Emotion

The developing ability to express a variety of feelings through facial expressions, movements, gestures, sounds, or words

8 months	18 months	36 months
At around eight months of age, children express a variety of primary emotions such as contentment, distress, joy, sadness, interest, surprise, disgust, anger, and fear. (Lamb, Bornstein, and Teti 2002, 341)	At around 18 months of age, children express emotions in a clear and intentional way, and begin to express some complex emotions, such as pride.	At around 36 months of age, children express complex, self-conscious emotions such as pride, embarrassment, shame, and guilt. Children demonstrate awareness of their feelings by using words to describe feelings to others or acting them out in pretend play. (Lewis and others 1989; Lewis 2000b; Lagattuta and Thompson 2007)
For example, the child may:	**For example, the child may:**	**For example, the child may:**
• Exhibit wariness, cry, or turn away when a stranger approaches. (6 mos.; Lamb, Bornstein, and Teti 2002, 338; Fogel 2001, 297; 7–8 mos.; Lewis 2000a, 277) • Be more likely to react with anger than just distress when accidentally hurt by another child. (later in the first year; Lamb, Bornstein, and Teti 2002, 341) • Express fear of unfamiliar people by moving near a familiar infant care teacher. (8 mos.; Bronson 1972) • Stop crying and snuggle after being picked up by a parent. • Show surprise when the infant care teacher removes the blanket covering her face to start a game of peek-a-boo.	• Show affection for a family member by hugging. (8–18 mos.; Lally and others 1995; Greenspan and Greenspan 1985, 84) • Express jealousy by trying to crowd onto the infant care teacher's lap when another child is already sitting there. (12–18 mos.; Hart and others 1998) • Express anger at having a toy taken away by taking it back out of the other child's hands or hitting her. (18 mos.; Squires, Bricker, and Twombly 2002, 115) • Smile directly at other children when interacting with them. (18 mos.; Squires, Bricker, and Twombly 2002, 115) • Express pride by communicating, "I did it!" (15–24 mos.; Lewis and others 1989; Lewis 2000b)	• Hide face with hands when feeling embarrassed. (Lagattuta and Thompson 2007) • Use words to describe feelings; for example, "I don't like that." (24–36 mos.; Fogel 2001, 414; 24–36 mos.; Harris and others 1989; Yuill 1984) • Communicate, "I miss Grandma," after talking on the phone with her. (24–36 mos.; Harris and others 1989; Yuill 1984) • Act out different emotions during pretend play by "crying" when pretending to be sad and "cooing" when pretending to be happy. (Dunn, Bretherton, and Munn 1987) • Express guilt after taking a toy out of another child's cubby without permission by trying to put it back without anyone seeing. (Lagattuta and Thompson 2007)

Chart continues on next page.

Expression of Emotion

Behaviors leading up to the foundation (4 to 7 months)	Behaviors leading up to the foundation (9 to 17 months)	Behaviors leading up to the foundation (19 to 35 months)
During this period, the child may:	During this period, the child may:	During this period, the child may:
• Get frustrated or angry when unable to reach a toy. (4–6 mos.; Sternberg, Campos, and Emde 1983) • Express joy by squealing. (5–6 mos.; Parks 2004, 125) • Frown and make noises to indicate frustration. (5–6 mos.; Parks 2004, 125) • Be surprised when something unexpected happens. (First 6 mos. of life; Lewis 2000a)	• Become anxious when a parent leaves the room. (6–9 mos.; Parks 2004) • Knock a shape-sorter toy away when it gets to be too frustrating. (10–12 mos.; Sroufe 1979) • Show anger, when another child takes a toy, by taking it back. (10–12 mos.; Sroufe 1979) • Express fear by crying upon hearing a dog bark loudly or seeing someone dressed in a costume. (10 mos.; Bronson 1972) • Express sadness by frowning after losing or misplacing a favorite toy. (9–10 mos.; Fogel 2001, 300) • Smile with affection as a sibling approaches. (10 mos.; Sroufe 1979; Fox and Davidson 1988) • Push an unwanted object away. (12 mos.; Squires, Bricker, and Twombly 2002, 114)	• Communicate, "Mama mad" after being told by the mother to stop an action. (28 mos.; Bretherton and others 1986) • Use one or a few words to describe feelings to the infant care teacher. (18–30 mos.; Bretherton and others 1986; Dunn 1987) • Express frustration through tantrums. (18–36 mos.; Pruett 1999, 148)

Foundation: Empathy

The developing ability to share in the emotional experiences of others

8 months	18 months	36 months
At around eight months of age, children demonstrate awareness of others' feelings by reacting to their emotional expressions.	At around 18 months of age, children change their behavior in response to the feelings of others even though their actions may not always make the other person feel better. Children show an increased understanding of the reason for another's distress and may become distressed by the other's distress. (14 mos.; Zahn-Waxler, Robinson, and Emde 1992; Thompson 1987; 24 mos.; Zahn-Waxler and Radke-Yarrow 1982, 1990)	At around 36 months of age, children understand that other people have feelings that are different from their own and can sometimes respond to another's distress in a way that might make that person feel better. (24–36 mos.; Hoffman 1982; 18 mos.; Thompson 1987, 135).
For example, the child may:	**For example, the child may:**	**For example, the child may:**
<ul><li>Stop playing and look at a child who is crying. (7 mos.; American Academy of Pediatrics 2004, 212)</li><li>Laugh when an older sibling or peer makes a funny face. (8 mos.; Meisels and others 2003)</li><li>Return the smile of the infant care teacher.</li><li>Grimace when another child cries. (Older than 6 mos.; Wingert and Brant 2005, 35)</li></ul>	<ul><li>Offer to help a crying playmate by bringing his own mother over. (13–15 mos.; Wingert and Brant 2005, 35)</li><li>Try to hug a crying peer. (18 mos.; Thompson 1987, 135)</li><li>Bring her own special blanket to a peer who is crying. (13–15 mos.; Wingert and Brant 2005, 35)</li><li>Become upset when another child throws a tantrum.</li><li>Gently pat a crying peer on his back, just like his infant care teacher did earlier in the day. (16 mos.; Bergman and Wilson 1984; Zahn-Waxler and others 1992)</li><li>Hit a child who is crying loudly.</li><li>Stop playing and look with concerned attention at a child who is screaming.</li><li>Move quickly away from a child who is crying loudly.</li></ul>	<ul><li>Do a silly dance in an attempt to make a crying peer smile. (24–36 mos.; Dunn 1988)</li><li>Communicate, "Lucas is sad because Isabel took his cup." (36 mos.; Harris and others 1989; Yuill 1984)</li><li>Comfort a younger sibling who is crying by patting his back, expressing "It's okay" and offering him a snack. (Denham 1998, 34)</li><li>Communicate, "Mama sad" when the mother cries during a movie. (24–36 mos.; Dunn 1994; Harris 2000, 282).</li><li>Communicate, "Olivia's mama is happy" and point to or indicate the illustration in the picture book. (24 mos.; Harris 2000, 282).</li><li>Get an infant care teacher to help a child who has fallen down and is crying.</li></ul>

Chart continues on next page.

Empathy

Behaviors leading up to the foundation (4 to 7 months)	Behaviors leading up to the foundation (9 to 17 months)	Behaviors leading up to the foundation (19 to 35 months)
During this period, the child may: • Cry when hearing another baby cry. (Younger than 6 mos; Wingert and Brant 2005, 35)	During this period, the child may: • Stand nearby and quietly watch a peer who has fallen down and is crying. • Exhibit social referencing by looking for emotional indicators in others' faces, voices, or gestures to decide what to do when uncertain. (10–12 mos.; Thompson 1987, 129) • Cry upon hearing another child cry. (12 mos.; Meisels and others 2003, 26)	During this period, the child may: • Hug a crying peer. (18–24 mos.; Parks 2004, 123) • Become upset in the presence of those who are upset.

Foundation: Emotion Regulation

The developing ability to manage emotional responses, with assistance from others and independently

8 months	18 months	36 months
At around eight months of age, children use simple behaviors to comfort themselves and begin to communicate the need for help to alleviate discomfort or distress.	At around 18 months of age, children demonstrate a variety of responses to comfort themselves and actively avoid or ignore situations that cause discomfort. Children can also communicate needs and wants through the use of a few words and gestures. (National Research Council and Institute of Medicine 2000, 112; 15–18 mos.; American Academy of Pediatrics 2004, 270; Coplan 1993, 1)	At around 36 months of age, children anticipate the need for comfort and try to prepare themselves for changes in routine. Children have many self-comforting behaviors to choose from, depending on the situation, and can communicate specific needs and wants. (Kopp 1989; CDE 2005)
For example, the child may:	**For example, the child may:**	**For example, the child may:**
• Turn away from an overstimulating activity. (3–12 mos.; Rothbart, Ziaie, and O'Boyle 1992) • Vocalize to get a parent's attention. (6.5–8 mos.; Parks 2004, 126) • Lift arms to the infant care teacher to communicate a desire to be held. (7–9 mos.; Coplan 1993, 3; 5–9 mos.; Parks 2004, 121) • Turn toward the infant care teacher for assistance when crying. (6–9 mos.; Fogel 2001, 274) • Cry after her hand was accidentally stepped on by a peer and then hold the hand up to the infant care teacher to look at it. • Reach toward a bottle that is up on the counter and vocalize when hungry. • Make a face of disgust to tell the infant care teacher that he does not want any more food. (6–9 mos.; Lerner and Ciervo 2003) • Bump head, cry, and look to infant care teacher for comfort. • Suck on a thumb to make self feel better. • Look at the infant care teacher when an unfamiliar person enters the room.	• Use gestures and simple words to express distress and seek specific kinds of assistance from the infant care teacher in order to calm self. (Brazelton 1992; Kopp 1989, 347) • Use comfort objects, such as a special blanket or stuffed toy, to help calm down. (Kopp 1989, 348) • Seek to be close to a parent when upset. (Lieberman 1993) • Play with a toy as a way to distract self from discomfort. (12–18 mos.; Kopp 1989, 347) • Communicate, "I'm okay" after falling down. (National Research Council and Institute of Medicine 2000, 112) • Indicate her knee and say "boo boo" after falling down and gesture or ask for a bandage. • Approach the infant care teacher for a hug and express, "Mommy work," then point to the door to communicate missing the mother.	• Reach for the mother's hand just before she pulls a bandage off the child's knee. • Ask the infant care teacher to hold him up to the window to wave good-bye before the parent leaves in the morning. • Show the substitute teacher that she likes a back rub during naptime by patting own back while lying on the mat. • Play quietly in a corner of the room right after drop-off, until ready to play with the other children. • Ask the infant care teacher to explain what's going to happen at the child's dental appointment later in the day. • Communicate, "Daddy always comes back" after saying good-bye to him in the morning.

Chart continues on next page.

Emotion Regulation

Behaviors leading up to the foundation (4 to 7 months)	Behaviors leading up to the foundation (9 to 17 months)	Behaviors leading up to the foundation (19 to 35 months)
During this period, the child may: • Suck on hands, focus on an interesting toy, or move the body in a rocking motion to calm self. (3–6 mos.; Parks 2004, 10) • Cry inconsolably less often than in the early months. (6 mos.; Parks 2004, 10) • Calm self by sucking on fingers or hands. (4 mos.; Thelen and Fogel 1989; 3–12 mos.; Bronson 2000b, 64) • Be able to inhibit some negative emotions. (Later in the first year; Fox and Calkins 2000) • Shift attention away from a distressing event onto an object, as a way of managing emotions. (6 mos.; Weinberg and others 1999) • Fall asleep when feeling overwhelmed.	During this period, the child may: • Move away from something that is bothersome and move toward the infant care teacher for comfort. (6–12 mos.; Bronson 2000b, 64) • Fight back tears when a parent leaves for the day. (12 mos.; Bridges, Grolnick, and Connell 1997; Parritz 1996; Sroufe 1979) • Look for a cue from the infant care teacher when unsure if something is safe. (10–12 mos.; Fogel 2001, 305; Dickstein and Parke 1988; Hirshberg and Svejda 1990) • Fuss to communicate needs or wants; begin to cry if the infant care teacher does not respond soon enough. (11–19 mos.; Hart and Risley 1999, 77) • Repeat sounds to get the infant care teacher's attention. (11–19 mos.; Hart and Risley 1999, 79)	During this period, the child may: • Continue to rely on adults for reassurance and help in controlling feelings and behavior. (Lally and others 1995) • Reenact emotional events in play to try to gain mastery over these feelings. (Greenspan and Greenspan 1985) • Use words to ask for specific help with regulating emotions. (Kopp 1989) • Express wants and needs verbally; for example, say, "hold me" to the infant care teacher when feeling tired or overwhelmed. (30–31.5 mos.; Parks 2004, 130)

Foundation: Impulse Control

The developing capacity to wait for needs to be met, to inhibit potentially hurtful behavior, and to act according to social expectations, including safety rules

8 months	18 months	36 months
At around eight months of age, children act on impulses. (Birth–9 mos.; Bronson 2000b, 64)	At around 18 months of age, children respond positively to choices and limits set by an adult to help control their behavior. (18 mos.; Meisels and others 2003, 34; Kaler and Kopp 1990)	At around 36 months of age, children may sometimes exercise voluntary control over actions and emotional expressions. (Bronson 2000b, 67)
For example, the child may:	**For example, the child may:**	**For example, the child may:**
• Explore the feel of hair by pulling it. (4–7 mos.; American Academy of Pediatrics 2004, 226) • Reach for an interesting toy that another child is mouthing. • Reach for another child's bottle that was just set down nearby. • Turn the head away or push the bottle away when finished eating (8 mos.; Meisels and others 2003, 19).	• Stop drawing on the wall when a parent asks. (18 mos.; Meisels and others 2003) • Choose one toy when the infant care teacher asks, "Which one do you want?" even though the child really wants both. • Express "no no" while approaching something the child knows she should not touch, because the infant care teacher has communicated "no no" in the past when the child tried to do this. • Look to the infant care teacher to see his reaction when the child reaches toward the light switch. • Stop reaching for the eyeglasses on the infant care teacher's face when she gently says, "no no." (Scaled score of 10 for 7:16–8:15 mos.; Bayley 2006, 87; 12 mos.; Meisels and others 2003, 27)	• Jump up and down on the couch but stop jumping and climb down when a parent enters the room. (36 mos.; Meisels and others 2003) • Experience difficulty (e.g., cry, whine, pout) with transitions. (30–36 mos.; Parks 2004, 320) • Begin to share. • Handle transitions better when prepared ahead of time or when the child has some control over what happens. • Touch a pet gently without needing to be reminded. • Wait to start eating until others at the table are also ready.

Chart continues on next page.

Impulse Control

Behaviors leading up to the foundation (4 to 7 months)	Behaviors leading up to the foundation (9 to 17 months)	Behaviors leading up to the foundation (19 to 35 months)
During this period, the child may: • Cry when hungry or tired. • Fall asleep when tired.	During this period, the child may: • Crawl too close to a younger infant lying nearby. • Refrain from exploring another baby's hair when reminded to be gentle. (8–10 mos.; Brazelton 1992, 256) • Look at the infant care teacher's face to determine whether it is all right to play with a toy on the table. (12 mos.; Meisels and others 2003, 25) • Bite another child who takes a toy. • Reach for food on a plate before the infant care teacher offers it. (12 mos.; Meisels and others 2003, 25)	During this period, the child may: • Begin to use words and dramatic play to describe, understand, and control impulses and feelings. (Lally and others 1995) • Communicate, "Mine!" and take a doll out of the hands of a peer. (23–24 mos.; Parks 2004, 330) • Throw a puzzle piece on the floor after having trouble fitting it in the opening. (24 mos.; Meisels and others 2003) • Open the playground door and run out, even after being asked by the infant care teacher to wait. (24 mos.; Meisels and others 2003) • Start to take another child's toy, then stop after catching the eye of the infant care teacher. (24 mos.; Meisels and others 2003) • Use a quiet voice at naptime. (30 mos.; Meisels and others 2003) • Understand and carry out simple commands or rules. (Bronson 2000b, 85) • Have a tantrum rather than attempt to manage strong feelings. (Brazelton 1992) • Be able to wait for a turn.

Foundation: Social Understanding

The developing understanding of the responses, communication, emotional expressions, and actions of other people

8 months	18 months	36 months
At around eight months of age, children have learned what to expect from familiar people, understand what to do to get another's attention, engage in back-and-forth interactions with others, and imitate the simple actions or facial expressions of others.	At around 18 months of age, children know how to get the infant care teacher to respond in a specific way through gestures, vocalizations, and shared attention; use another's emotional expressions to guide their own responses to unfamiliar events; and learn more complex behavior through imitation. Children also engage in more complex social interactions and have developed expectations for a greater number of familiar people.	At around 36 months of age, children can talk about their own wants and feelings and those of other people, describe familiar routines, participate in coordinated episodes of pretend play with peers, and interact with adults in more complex ways.
For example, the child may:	**For example, the child may:**	**For example, the child may:**
• Smile when the infant care teacher pauses, to get her to continue playing peek-a-boo or pat-a-cake. • Squeal in anticipation of the infant care teacher's uncovering her eyes during a game of peek-a-boo. • Learn simple behaviors by imitating a parent's facial expressions, gestures, or sounds. • Try to get a familiar game or routine started by prompting the infant care teacher. • Quiet crying upon realizing that the infant care teacher is approaching.	• Gesture toward a desired toy or food while reaching, making imperative vocal sounds, and looking toward the infant care teacher. • Seek reassurance from the infant care teacher when unsure about something. • Vary response to different infant care teachers depending on their play styles, even before they have started playing; for example, get very excited upon seeing an infant care teacher who regularly plays in an exciting, vigorous manner. • Engage in back-and-forth play that involves turn-taking, such as rolling a ball back and forth. • Look in the direction of the infant care teacher's gesturing or pointing. • Learn more complex behaviors through imitation, such as watching an older child put toys together and then doing it.	• Name own feelings or desires, explicitly contrast them with another's, or describe why the child feels the way he does. • Describe what happens during the bedtime routine or another familiar everyday event. • Move into and out of pretend play roles, tell other children what they should do in their roles, or extend the sequence (such as by asking "Wanna drink?" after bringing a pretend hamburger to the table as a waiter). • Help the infant care teacher for a missing toy. • Talk about what happened a recent past experience, assistance of the infant ca • Help the infant care teacher up at the end of the day by the toys in the usual places

Chart continues on next page.

Social Understanding

Behaviors leading up to the foundation (4 to 7 months)	Behaviors leading up to the foundation (9 to 17 months)	Behaviors leading up to the foundation (19 to 35 months)
During this period, the child may: • Make imperative vocal sounds to attract the infant care teacher's attention. • Participate in playful, face-to-face interactions with an adult, such as taking turns vocalizing.	During this period, the child may: • Follow the infant care teacher's gaze to look at a toy. • Hold up or gesture toward objects in order to direct the infant care teacher's attention to them.	During this period, the child may: • Vary play with different peers depending on their preferred play activities. • Imitate the behavior of peers as well as adults.

References

Ainsworth, M. D. 1967. *Infancy in Uganda: Infant Care and the Growth of Love.* Baltimore: Johns Hopkins University Press.

American Academy of Pediatrics. 2004. *Caring for Your Baby and Young Child: Birth to Age 5* (Fourth edition). Edited by S. P. Shelov and R. E. Hannemann. New York: Bantam Books.

Anderson, C., and D. Keltner. 2002. "The Role of Empathy in the Formation and Maintenance of Social Bonds." *Behavioral and Brain Sciences* 25(1): 21–22.

Barrera, M. E., and D. Maurer. 1981. "Discrimination of Strangers by the Three Month-Old." *Child Development* 52(2): 558–63.

Barrett, L., and others. 2007. "The Experience of Emotion." *Annual Review of Psychology* 58:373–403.

Bates, E. 1990. "Language About Me and You: Pronominal Reference and the Emerging Concept of Self," in *The Self in Transition: Infancy to Childhood.* Edited by D. Cicchetti and M. Beeghly. Chicago: University of Chicago Press.

Bayley, N. 2006. *Bayley Scales of Infant and Toddler Development* (Third edition). San Antonio, TX: Harcourt Assessment, Inc.

Bell, M., and C. Wolfe. 2004. "Emotion and Cognition: An Intricately Bound Developmental Process." *Child Development* 75(2): 366–70.

Bergman, A., and A. Wilson. 1984. "Thoughts About Stages on the Way to Empathy and the Capacity for Concern," in *Empathy II.* Edited by J. Lichtenberg, M. Bornstein, and D. Silver. Hillsdale, NJ: Lawrence Erlbaum Associates.

Brazelton, T. B. 1992. *Touchpoints: Your Child's Emotional and Behavioral Development.* New York: Perseus Publishing.

———. 1998. "How to Help Parents of Young Children: The Touchpoints Model." *Clinical Child Psychology and Psychiatry. Special Issue: Parenting* 3(3): 481–3.

Brazelton, T. B., and J. D. Sparrow. 2006. *Touchpoints: Your Child's Emotional and Behavioral Development, Birth to 3.* Cambridge, MA: Da Capo Press.

Bretherton, I., and others. 1986. "Learning to Talk About Emotions: A Functionalist Perspective." *Child Development* 57:529–48.

Bridges, L. J., W. S. Grolnick, and J. P Connell. 1997. "Infant Emotion Regulation with Mothers and Fathers." *Infant Behavior and Development* 20:47–57.

Bronson, G. W. 1972. "Infants' Reaction to Unfamiliar Persons and Novel Objects," *Monographs of the Society for Research in Child Development* 37(148): 1–46.

Bronson, M. 2000a. "Recognizing and Supporting the Development of Self-Regulation in Young Children." *Young Children* 55(2): 32–37.

———. 2000b. *Self-Regulation in Early Childhood: Nature and Nurture.* New York: Guilford Press.

Bullock, M., and P. Lutkenhaus. 1988. "The Development of Volitional Behavior in the Toddler Years." *Child Development* 59:664–74.

———. 1990. "Who Am I? Self-Understanding in Toddlers." *Merrill-Palmer Quarterly* 36:217–38.

Burk, D. I. 1996. "Understanding Friendship and Social Interaction." *Childhood Education* 72(5): 282–85.

Cacioppo, J., and G. Berntson. 1999. "The Affect System: Architecture and Operating Characteristics." *Current Directions in Psychological Science* 8(5): 133–37.

California Department of Education (CDE). 2005. "Desired Results Developmental Profile (DRDP)." http://www.cde.ca.gov/sp/cd/ci/desiredresults.asp (accessed February 7, 2007). Sacramento: California Department of Education.

California Department of Education and WestEd Center for Child and Family Studies. 2009. *California Infant/Toddler Learning and Development Foundations.* Sacramento: California Department of Education.

Campos, J., C. Frankel, and L. Camras. 2004. "On the Nature of Emotion Regulation." *Child Development* 75(2): 377–94.

Caufield, R. 1995. "Reciprocity Between Infants and Caregivers During the First Year of Life." *Early Childhood Education Journal* 23(1): 3–8.

Cheah, C., and K. Rubin. 2003. "European American and Mainland Chinese Mothers' Socialization Beliefs Regarding Preschoolers' Social Skills." *Parenting: Science and Practice* 3(1): 1–21.

Cohen, J., and others. 2005. *Helping Young Children Succeed: Strategies to Promote Early Childhood Social and Emotional Development.* Washington, DC: National Conference of State Legislatures and Zero to Three.

Connell, J. P. 1990. "Context, Self, and Action: A Motivational Analysis of Self-System Processes Across the Lifespan," in *The Self in Transition: Infancy to Childhood.* Edited by D. Cicchetti and Coplan, J. 1993. Early Language Milestone Scale: Examiner's Manual (Second edition). Austin, TX: Pro-ed.

Cost, Quality & Child Outcomes Study Team. 1995. *Cost, Quality and Child Outcomes in Child Care Centers: Executive Summary.* Denver: University of Colorado, Economics Department.

Davies, D. 2004. *Child Development: A Practitioner's Guide* (Second edition). New York: Guilford Press.

DeCasper, A. J., and W. P. Fifer. 1980. "Of Human Bonding: Newborns Prefer Their Mothers' Voices." *Science* 208(6): 1174–76.

Denham, S. A. 1998. *Emotional Development in Young Children.* New York: Guilford Press.

Denham, S. A., and R. Weissberg. 2003. "Social-Emotional Learning in Early Childhood: What We Know and Where to Go From Here," in *A Blueprint for the Promotion of Prosocial Behavior in Early Childhood.* Edited by E.

Chesebrough and others. New York: Kluwer Academic/Plenum Publishers.

Dickstein, S., and R. D. Parke. 1988. "Social Referencing in Infancy: A Glance at Fathers and Marriage," *Child Development* 59(2): 506–11.

Dunn, J. 1983. "Sibling Relationships in Early Childhood." *Child Development* 54(4): 787–811.

———. 1987. "The Beginnings of Moral Understanding: Development in the Second Year," in *The Emergence of Morality in Young Children.* Edited by J. Kagan and S. Lamb. Chicago: University of Chicago Press.

———. 1988. *The Beginnings of Social Understanding.* Cambridge, MA: Harvard University Press.

———. 1994. "Changing Minds and Changing Relationships," in *Children's Early Understanding of Mind: Origins and Development.* Edited by C. Lewis and P. Mitchell. Hillsdale, NJ: Lawrence Erlbaum Associates.

Dunn, J., I. Bretherton, and P. Munn. 1987. "Conversations About Feeling States Between Mothers and Their Young Children." *Developmental Psychology* 23(1): 132–39.

Eisenberg, N. 2000. "Emotion, Regulation and Moral Development." *Annual Review of Psychology* 51:665–97.

Eisenberg, N., and others. 1993. "The Relations of Emotionality and Regulation to Preschoolers' Social Skills and Sociometric Status." *Child Development* 64:1418–38.

Eisenberg, N., C. Champion, and Y. Ma. 2004. "Emotion-Related Regulation: An Emerging Construct." *Merrill-Palmer Quarterly* 50(3): 236–59.

Eisenberg, N., and T. Spinrad. 2004. "Emotion-Related Regulation: Sharpening the Definition." *Child Development* 75(2): 334–39.

Fabes, R., and others. 2001. "Preschoolers' Spontaneous Emotion Vocabulary:

Relations to Likability." *Early Education & Development* 12(1): 11–27.

Fernald, A. 1993. "Approval and Disapproval: Infant Responsiveness to Vocal Affect in Familiar and Unfamiliar Languages." *Child Development* 64(3): 657–74.

Fogel, A. 2001. *Infancy: Infant, Family, and Society* (Fourth edition). Belmont, CA: Wadsworth/Thomson Learning.

Fox, N. A., and S. D. Calkins. 2000. "Multiple Measure Approaches to the Study of Infant Emotion," in *Handbook of Emotions* (Second edition). Edited by M. Lewis and J. M. Haviland-Jones. New York: Guilford Press.

———. 2003. "The Development of Self-control of Emotion: Intrinsic and Extrinsic Influences."
Motivation and Emotion 27(1): 7–26.

Fox, N. A., and R. J. Davidson. 1988. "Patterns of Brain Electrical Activity During the Expression of Discrete Emotions in Ten-Month-Old Infants." *Developmental Psychology* 24:230–36.

Fraiberg, S. H. 1959. *The Magic Years.* New York: Fireside.

Frankenburg, W. K., and others. 1990. *Denver II Screening Manual.* Denver, CO: Denver Developmental Materials.

Fredrickson, B. 2000. "Cultivating Positive Emotions to Optimize Health and Well-Being." *Prevention and Treatment* 3(1).

———. 2003. "The Value of Positive Emotions." *American Scientist* 91: 330–35.

Greenspan, S., and N. T. Greenspan. 1985. *First Feelings: Milestones in the Emotional Development of Your Baby and Child.* New York: Penguin Books.

Greven, Phillip. 1988. *The Protestant Temperament: Patterns of Child-Rearing, Religious Experience, and the Self in Early America.* Chicago: University of Chicago Press.

Gustafson, G. E., J. A. Green, and M. J. West. 1979. "The Infant's Changing Role in Mother-Infant Games: The Growth of Social Skills." *Infant Behavior and Development* 2:301–8.

Harris, P. L. 2000. "Understanding Emotion," in *Handbook of Emotions* (Second edition). Edited by M. Lewis and J. M. Haviland-Jones. New York: Guilford Press.

Harris, P. L., and others. 1989. "Young Children's Theory of Mind and Emotion." *Cognition and Emotion* 3(4): 379–400.

Hart, B., and T. R. Risley. 1999. *The Social World of Children: Learning to Talk.* Baltimore, MD: Paul H. Brookes Publishing.

Hart, S., and others. 1998. "Jealousy Protests in Infants of Depressed Mothers." *Infant Behavior and Development* 21(1): 137–48.

Hay, D. F., J. Pederson, and A. Nash. 1982. "Dyadic Interaction in the First Year of Life," in *Peer Relationships and Social Skills in Childhood.* Edited by K. H. Rubin and H. S. Rossi. New York: Springer Verlag.

Hirshberg, L. M., and M. Svejda. 1990. "When Infants Look to Their Parents: Infants' Social Referencing of Mothers Compared to Fathers." *Child Development* 61(4): 1175–86.

Hoffman, M. L. 1982. "Development of Pro-social Motivation: Empathy and Guilt," in *The Development of Prosocial Behavior.* Edited by N. Eisenberg. New York: Academic Press.

Howes, C. 1983. "Patterns of Friendship." *Child Development* 54(4): 1041–53.

———. 1987. "Social Competence with Peers in Young Children: Developmental Sequences." *Developmental Review* 7: 252–72.

———. 1988. "Peer Interaction of Young Children." Monographs of the Society for Research in *Child Development* 53(1).

Howes, C., and C. C. Matheson. 1992. "Sequences in the Development of Competent Play with Peers: Social and Social Pretend Play." *Developmental Psychology* 28(5): 961–74.

Johnson, M., and others. 1991. "Newborns' Preferential Tracking of Face-Like Stimuli and Its Subsequent Decline." *Cognition* 40(1–2): 1–19.

Johnstone, T., and K. R. Scherer. 2000. "Vocal Communication of Emotion," in *Handbook of Emotions* (Second edition). Edited by M. Lewis and J. Haviland-Jones. New York: Guilford Press.

Kaler, S. R., and C. B. Kopp. 1990. "Compliance and Comprehension in Very Young Toddlers." *Child Development* 61(6): 1997–2003.

Kaye, K., and A. Fogel. 1980. "The Temporal Structure of Face-to-Face Communication Between Mothers and Infants." *Developmental Psychology* 16:454–64.

Klages, Mary. Lectures on Jacques Lacan. http://www.colorado.edu/English/courses/ENGL2012Klages/lacan.html.

Knox, J., and J. Wright. 1977. A Letter from the Vatican: March 31, 1977, First Penance, First Communion.

Kontos, S., and A. Wilcox-Herzog. January, 1997. "Research in Review: Teacher's Interactions with Children: Why Are They So Important?" *Young Children* 52(2): 4–12.

Kopp, C. 1989. "Regulation of Distress and Negative Emotions: A Developmental View." *Developmental Psychology* 25(3): 343–54.

Kravitz, H., D. Goldenberg, and A. Neyhus. 1978. "Tactual Exploration by Normal Infants." *Developmental Medicine and Child-Neurology* 20(6): 720–26.

Lagattuta, K. H., and R. A. Thompson. 2007. "The Development of Self-Conscious Emotions: Cognitive Processes and Social Influences," in *The Self-Conscious Emotions: Theory and Research*. Edited by J. L. Tracy, R. W. Robins, and J. P. Tangney. New York: Guilford Press.

Lally, J. R., and others. 1995. *Caring for Infants and Toddlers in Groups: Developmentally Appropriate Practice*. Washington, DC: Zero to Three Press.

Lamb, M. E., M. H. Bornstein, and D. M. Teti. 2002. *Development in Infancy: An Introduction* (Fourth edition). Mahwah, NJ: Lawrence Erlbaum Associates.

Lerner, C., and L. A. Ciervo. 2003. *Healthy Minds: Nurturing Children's Development from 0 to 36 Months*. Washington, DC: Zero to Three Press and American Academy of Pediatrics.

Lerner, C., and A. L. Dombro. 2000. *Learning and Growing Together: Understanding and Supporting Your Child's Development*. Washington, DC: Zero to Three Press.

Levenson, R., and A. Ruef. 1992. "Empathy: A Physiological Substrate." *Journal of Personality and Social Psychology* 63(2): 234–46.

Levine, L. E. 1983. "Mine: Self-Definition in 2-Year-Old Boys." *Developmental Psychology* 19:544–49.

Lewis, M. 2000a. "The Emergence of Human Emotions," in *Handbook of Emotions* (Second edition). Edited by M. Lewis and J. M. Haviland-Jones. New York: Guilford Press.

———. 2000b. "Self-Conscious Emotions: Embarrassment, Pride, Shame, and Guilt," in *Handbook of Emotions* (Second edition). Edited by M. Lewis and J. M. Haviland-Jones. New York: Guilford Press.

Lewis, M., S. M. Alessandri, and M. W. Sullivan. 1992. "Differences in Shame and Pride as a Function of Children's Gender and Task Difficulty." *Child Development* 63(3): 630–38.

Lewis, M., and J. Brooks-Gunn. 1979. *Social Cognition and the Acquisition of Self*. New York: Plenum Press.

Lewis, M., and others. 1989. "Self Development and Self-Conscious Emotions." *Child Development* 60(1): 146–56.

Lieberman, A. F. 1993. *The Emotional Life of the Toddler*. New York: Free Press.

Locke, John. 1690 "An Essay Concerning Human Understanding: Book I." In *An Essay Concerning Human Understanding* (1689), 38th edition. London; William Tegg.

Marvin, R., and P. Britner. 1999. "Normative Development: The Ontogeny of Attachment," in *Handbook of Attachment: Theory, Research, and Clinical Applications.* Edited by J. Cassidy and P. Shaver. New York: Guilford Press.

McCarty, M. E., R. K. Clifton, and R. R. Collard. 1999. "Problem Solving in Infancy: The Emergence of an Action Plan," *Developmental Psychology* 35(4): 1091–101.

Meisels, S. J., and others. 2003. *The Ounce Scale: Standards for the Developmental Profiles (Birth–42 Months).* New York: Pearson Early Learning.

Melson, G., and A. Cohen. 1981. "Contextual Influences on Children's Activity: Sex Differences in Effects of Peer Presence and Interpersonal Attraction." *Genetic Psychology Monographs* 103: 243–60.

Mesquita, B., and N. Frijda. 1992. "Cultural Variations in Emotions: A Review." *Psychological Bulletin* 112(2): 179–204.

Messinger, D., and A. Fogel. 2007. "The Interactive Development of Social Smiling," in *Advances in Child Development and Behavior* 35. Edited by R. V. Kail. Burlington, MA: Elsevier.

Mueller, E., and T. Lucas. 1975. "A Developmental Analysis of Peer Interaction Among Toddlers," in *Friendship and Peer Relations.* Edited by M. Lewis and L. Rosenblum. New York: Wiley.

National Research Council and Institute of Medicine. 2000. *From Neurons to Neighborhoods: The Science of Early Childhood Development.* Committee on Integrating the Science of Early Childhood Development. Edited by J. P. Shonkoff and D. A. Phillips. Board on Children, Youth and Families, Commission on Behavioral and Social Sciences and Education. Washington, DC: National Academy Press.

National Scientific Council on the Developing Child. 2004. "Children's Emotional Development Is Built into the Architecture of Their Brains." Working Paper No. 2. http://www.developingchild.net (accessed December 5, 2006). Cambridge, MA: Center on the Developing Child at Harvard University.

NICHD Early Child Care Research Network. 1996. "Characteristics of Infant Child Care: Factors Contributing to Positive Caregiving." *Early Childhood Research Quarterly* 11(3): 269–306.

Panksepp, J. 2001. "The Long-Term Psychobiological Consequences of Infant Emotions: Prescriptions for the Twenty-First Century." *Infant Mental Health Journal* 22(1–2): 132–73.

Parks, S. 2004. *Inside HELP: Hawaii Early Learning Profile Administration and Reference Manual.* Palo Alto, CA: VORT Corporation.

Parritz, R. H. 1996. "A Descriptive Analysis of Toddler Coping in Challenging Circumstances." *Infant Behavior and Development* 19:171–80.

Pruett, K. D. 1999. *Me, Myself and I: How Children Build Their Sense of Self (18 to 36 Months).* New York: Goddard Press.

Quann, V., and C. Wien. 2006. "The Visible Empathy of Infants and Toddlers." *Young Children* 61(4): 22–29.

Raikes, H. 1996. "A Secure Base for Babies: Applying Attachment Concepts to the Infant Care Setting." *Young Children* 51(5): 59–67.

Raver, C. 2002. "Emotions Matter: Making the Case for the Role of Young Children's Emotional Development for Early School Readiness." *SRCD Social Policy Report* 16(3).

Ross, H. S., and B. D. Goldman. 1977. "Establishing New Social Relations in Infancy," in *Attachment Behavior.* Edited by T. Alloway, P. Pliner, and L. Krames. New York: Plenum Press.

Rothbart, M. K., H. Ziaie, and C. G. O'Boyle. 1992. "Self-Regulation and Emotion in Infancy," in *Emotion and Its Regulation in Early Development* (No. 55). Edited by N. Eisenberg and

R. Fabes. San Francisco: Jossey-Bass/ Pfeiffer.

Rubin, K. H., and H. S. Rossi, eds. *Peer Relationships and Social Skills in Childhood.* New York: Springer-Verlag.

Ryalls, B., R. Gul, and K. Ryalls. 2000. "Infant Imitation of Peer and Adult Models: Evidence for a Peer Model Advantage." *Merrill-Palmer Quarterly* 46(1): 188–202.

Saarni, C., and others. 2006. "Emotional Development: Action, Communication, and Understanding," in *Handbook of Child Psychology* (Sixth edition), *Vol. 3, Social, Emotional, and Personality Development.* Edited by N. Eisenberg. Hoboken, NJ: John Wiley and Sons.

Scaramella, L. V., and L. D. Leve. 2004. "Clarifying Parent-Child Reciprocities During Early Childhood: The Early Childhood Coercion Model." *Clinical Child and Family Psychology Review* 7(2): 89–107.

Schaffer, H. R., and P. E. Emerson. 1964. "The Development of Social Attachments in Infancy." *Monographs of the Society for Research in Child Development* 29(3).

Segal, M. 2004. "The Roots and Fruits of Pretending," in *Children's Play: The Roots of Reading.* Edited by E. F. Zigler, D. G. Singer, and S. J. Bishop-Josef. Washington, DC: Zero to Three Press.

Shonkoff, J. P. 2004. *Science, Policy and the Developing Child: Closing the Gap Between What We Know and What We Do.* Washington, DC: Ounce of Prevention Fund.

Siegel, D. J. 1999. *The Developing Mind: How Relationships and the Brain Interact to Shape Who We Are.* New York: Guilford Press.

Silber, K. 1965. Pestalozzi: *The Man and His Work* (Second edition). London: Routledge and Kegan Paul.

Squires, J., D. Bricker, and E. Twombly. 2002. *The Ages & Stages Questionnaires: Social-Emotional. A Parent-Completed Child-Monitoring System for Social-Emotional Behaviors ASQ:SE.* User's Guide. Baltimore, MD: Paul H. Brookes Publishing.

Sroufe, L. A. 1979. "Socioemotional Development," in *Handbook of Infant Development.* Edited by J. Osofsky. New York: Wiley.

Stern, D. N. 1985. *The Interpersonal World of the Infant: A View from Psychoanalysis and Developmental Psychology.* New York: Basic Books.

Sternberg, C. R., J. J. Campos, and R. N. Emde. 1983. "The Facial Expression of Anger in Seven-Month-Old Infants." *Child Development* 54:178–84.

Stipek, D. J., J. H. Gralinski, and C. B. Kopp. 1990. "Self-Concept Development in the Toddler Years." *Developmental Psychology* 26(6): 972–77.

Suizzo, M., W. Chen, C. Cheng, A. S. Liang, H. Contreras, D. Zanger, and C. Robinson. 2008. "Parental Beliefs About Young Children's Socialization Across US Ethnic Groups: Coexistence of Independence and Interdependence." *Early Child Development and Care* 178(5): 467–86.

Taumoepeau, M., and T. Ruffman. 2008. "Stepping Stones to Others' Minds: Maternal Talk Relates to Child Mental State Language and Emotion Understanding at 15, 24, and 33 Months." *Child Development* 79(2): 284–302.

Teti, D. M. 1999. "Conceptualizations of Disorganization in the Preschool Years: An Integration," in *Attachment Disorganization.* Edited by J. Solomon and C. George. New York: Guilford Press.

Thelen, E., and A. Fogel. 1989. "Toward an Action-Based Theory of Infant Development," in *Action in Social Context: Perspectives on Early Development.* Edited by J. Lockman and N. Hazen. New York: Plenum Press.

Thompson, R. A. 1987. "Empathy and Emotional Understanding: The Early Development of Empathy," in *Empathy and Its Development.* Edited by N. Eisenberg and J. Strayer. New York: Cambridge University Press.

———. 2006. "The Development of the Person: Social Understanding, Relationships, Self, Conscience," in *Handbook of Child Psychology* (Sixth edition), *Volume 3: Social, Emotional, and Personality Development.* Edited by N. Eisenberg. Hoboken, NJ: Wiley and Sons.

Thompson, R. A., and R. Goodvin. 2005. "The Individual Child: Temperament, Emotion, Self and Personality," in *Developmental Science: An Advanced Textbook* (Fifth edition). Edited by M. H. Bornstein and M. E. Lamb. Mahwah, NJ: Lawrence Erlbaum Associates.

Tronick, E. Z. 1989. "Emotions and Emotional Communication in Infants." *American Psychologist* 44(2): 112–19.

Tsai, J., B. Knutson, and H. Fung. 2006. "Cultural Variation in Affect Valuation." *Journal of Personality and Social Psychology* 90(2): 288–307.

Tsai, J., R. Levenson, and K. McCoy. 2006. "Cultural and Temperamental Variation in Emotional Response." *Emotion* 6(3): 484–97.

Tsai, J., and others. 2007. "Learning What Feelings to Desire: Socialization of Ideal Affect Through Children's Storybooks," *Personality and Social Psychology Bulletin* 33(1): 17–30.

Weinberg, M. K., and others. 1999. "Gender Differences in Emotional Expressivity and Self-Regulation During Early Infancy." *Developmental Psychology* 35(1): 175–88.

Wellman, H. M., and K. H. Lagattuta. 2000. "Developing Understandings of Mind," in *Understanding Other Minds: Perspectives from Developmental Cognitive Neuroscience.* Edited by S. Baron-Cohen, T. Tager-Flusberg, and D. J. Cohen. New York: Oxford University Press.

Wingert, P., and M. Brant. 2005. "Reading Your Baby's Mind." *Newsweek* (August 15, 2005): 32–39.

Yuill, N. 1984. "Young Children's Coordination of Motive and Outcome in Judgments of Satisfaction and Morality." *British Journal of Developmental Psychology* 2:73–81.

Zahn-Waxler, C., and M. Radke-Yarrow. 1982. "The Development of Altruism: Alternative Research Strategies," in *The Development of Prosocial Behavior.* Edited by N. Eisenberg. New York: Academic Press.

———. 1990. "The Origins of Empathetic Concern." *Motivation and Emotion* 14: 107–30.

Zahn-Waxler, C., and others. 1992. "Development of Concern for Others." *Developmental Psychology* 28(1): 126–36.

Zahn-Waxler, C., J. Robinson, and R. Emde. 1992. "Development of Empathy in Twins." *Developmental Psychology* 28(6): 1038–47.

Zero to Three. 2004. "Infant and Early Childhood Mental Health: Promoting Healthy Social and Emotional Development." Fact Sheet, May 18, 2004. Washington, DC: Zero to Three. http://www. zerotothree.org/policy/ (accessed December 7, 2006).

OSP 11 122843

10-010 PR10-0013 05-11 10M